George Washington's 'Magick Money Man'

HARLOW GILES UNGER

NEW YORK TIMES BESTSELLING AUTHOR

Table of Contents

About the Author

HARLOW GILES UNGER is an award-winning journalist, broadcaster, educator, and renowned historian. A *New York Times Bestselling author* of thirty books, he is a former Distinguished Visiting Fellow in American History at George Washington's Mount Vernon. Among his books, *Lafayette* won the American Revolution Round Table Book Prize among other awards. His best-seller, *The Last Founding Father: James Monroe and a Nation's Call to Greatness*, earned the author a *Washington Post* designation as a Premier Presidential Biographer.

OTHER TITLES BY HARLOW GILES UNGER

American Tempest: How the Boston Tea Party Sparked a Revolution

Dr. Benjamin Rush: The Founding Father Who Healed a Wounded Nation

First Founding Father: Richard Henry Lee and the Call to Independence

John Hancock: Merchant King and American Patriot

John Quincy Adams

Lafayette

The Last Founding Father: James Monroe and A Nation's Call to Greatness

Lion of Liberty: Patrick Henry and the Call to a New Nation

Thomas Paine and the Clarion Call for American Independence

INTRODUCTION

B

ritish troops had all but annihilated George Washington's Continental Army in 1776 and they seized Philadelphia, the unofficial capital of the self-proclaimed United States of America the following year, all but ending America' struggle for independence.

The remnants of Washington's rebel troops fled to a barren mountain top in Valley Forge, Pennsylvania, where they faced a winter of starvation, frost bite, and death.

Besides a lack of food and water to sustain his troops, Washington had no funds to buy them ammunition, weapons, or even clothing, let alone pay them. As winter set in, his men faced starvation, frost-bite, and death. Without weapons to defend themselves, they began deserting.

But just as desertions threatened to end the American Revolution, a fat man from Philadelphia appeared in Washington's tent and, as if by magic—or "magick," as Washington spelled it—he produced the money to pay the troops and buy them enough clothing and arms to last the winter. His name was Robert Morris, Jr.; Washington called him his "magick money man."

Robert Morris, Jr. was America's richest man in 1776. The stroke of his pen sent waves of currencies and coins bounding over oceans, lapping every shore, spilling in and out of vaults, enriching merchants, planters, friends, family—and above all Robert Morris himself. His money bought and sold gold, silver, tea, tobacco, grain, iron ore, timber, cotton, silks and satins, silverware, china, foodstuffs, fine wines, furniture, cannons, cannon balls, rifles, slaves, and land—millions of acres of land—often without his personally taking possession of any tea, tobacco or anything else his fleet of ships carried.

What Robert Morris, Jr., did acquire was money—*capital*—lots of it; more than any other American in history at the time. While others bought, sold, and stored *things*, Morris bought, sold, and stored *capital*—borrowing more

when he thought it profitable, lending it if that seemed even more profitable, or reinvesting it to increase still more. His capital financed traffic in every imaginable commodity on his fleet of ships—the world's largest privately owned fleet, including the first American ships to trade with China.

To safeguard his capital and speed its flow around the universe, he founded America's first national bank to hold, invest, or lend money, and he laid the foundation of American free enterprise and capitalism. At the time, capital holdings went untouched and unfettered by government interference of any sort.

In effect, Morris invented capitalism and transformed the American economy into the richest, most prosperous the world ever saw.

In an even more important investment, however, Robert Morris used his capital to enhance America's political liberties by financing George Washington's Continental Army in the American War of Independence. Morris was not only a daring American capitalist, he was a daring American patriot, risking his life with fifty-five other intrepid Founding Fathers who signed the Declaration of Independence—a treasonous act in British America, punishable by death. Morris then risked his business, his fleet of ships, his three palatial homes, and his personal fortune to purchase and smuggle military supplies for the troops in Washington's army to free thirteen North American colonies from British rule.

Driven when pursuing wealth, Morris was one of the most easy-going Founding Fathers in a tavern or at home—warm, jolly, hospitable, a loving husband, doting father of seven, and an unswervingly loyal friend. With his wife Mary, he welcomed an endless parade of American and foreign notables to his mansions in Philadelphia and the nearby countryside along the beautiful Schuylkill River.

Their most frequent visitors—indeed, their closest friends—were George and Martha Washington, with whom private suppers together saw Mary and Martha giggle together like school-aged sisters. Though Washington's false teeth pained him too much to giggle, he and Robert were equally close and they and their wives often spent holidays together fishing or hunting.

Born in Liverpool, England's waterfront slums in 1734, Morris sailed to America when he was thirteen. With no formal education, he labored on Philadelphia's docks at first, worked his way into his employer's counting house, educated himself in Benjamin Franklin's library, and gradually mastered every element of domestic and international trade.

With eyes and ears absorbing every sight and sound on the piers, Morris discovered a trading flaw that would make him rich: why, he asked, spend capital one day to acquire and store goods you plan to sell the next day? Answering his own question, he defied principles of what was then the world's governing economic system—mercantilism—with a new way of doing business—a system the world now calls capitalism.

The economic foundation of the world's autocracies at the time relied on acquisition of resources by conquest. In that way, autocrats and royal despots exhausted national treasuries and men's lives to acquire the wealth of captured lands and enslaving the masses in fields and mines—all, to enrich themselves and a small coterie of royal families, noblemen, and churchmen.

Robert Morris undermined mercantilism with a more efficient, less costly type of trade that dispensed with wars of conquest and used capital instead of cannons to amass national and private wealth. Instead of accumulating and storing resources, he sold or traded them—often, before he even owned them—freeing ever more capital to amass ever more wealth.

In the end, Morris's economic machinations stripped the British crown of its dominion over American wealth and resources and allowed American free enterprise to stage an industrial revolution that would make the United States and the American people the richest on earth.

A hugely popular figure in Philadelphia, Morris was a member of the Continental Congress, where he was one of only two Founding Fathers who signed all three of the nation's founding documents—the Declaration of Independence, Articles of Confederation, and Constitution.

Elected Superintendent of Finance by the Continental Congress, Morris spent tens of millions of his own money to feed, clothe, and arm Washington's troops when they faced starvation in the arctic winter of 1777 at Valley Forge. When he exhausted his own money, he teamed with money broker Haym Solomon to work the financial miracle that produced Washington's military miracle at Yorktown. Washington called it "art magick." By war's end, Robert Morris had made the greatest personal financial sacrifice of any Founding Father and contributed more to winning American independence than anyone except George Washington.

The years after Yorktown saw a surge in demand for unsettled lands in the American West. Tens of thousands of European farmers and artisans fled poverty and Old World bondage for New World opportunities in America's unpeopled plains and forests. Western land values doubled, tripled, quadrupled.... Morris invested his every last *sou,* buying upwards of 10 million acres, becoming America's largest land owner. Other Founding Fathers joined him, including his friend George Washington, who bought 60,000 acres. With Morris, they envisioned millions migrating across the American continent, building towns, cities, roads, canals, and businesses.

To convert his and their visions into reality, Morris used his wit, wile, and wealth to coax the Constitutional Convention to strip states of power over interstate commerce and allow people, capital, and goods to flow freely across state lines in a new and then-unique economic common market, devoid of internal import-export duties and government controls.

In the century that followed, the American common market that Morris created, with its ever increasing territory and population, evolved into history's richest, most productive economic empire.

Neither Morris nor Washington would profit from that empire however. A decade-long war between Britain and France suddenly halted the flow of European emigrants across the Atlantic to America and all-but-ended demand for land in the West. Land prices collapsed, dragging Morris into bankruptcy. After a fierce gun fight at the entrance to the Morris country home, a sheriff's posse crashed through the door and dragged the king of capitalism to debtor's prison.

When his friend George Washington visited him in his prison cell, however, he found Morris undeterred. Beaming with optimism, Morris reminded Washington, "My dear General, I can never do things in the small. I must either be a man or a mouse." As he had been throughout his life, Morris remained determined to write another chapter in one of the most remarkable and thoroughly American rags-to-riches stories.

A model for poor immigrants in the century that followed, the life of Robert Morris depicts the dramatic rise of an intrepid, penniless, immigrant boy to success, incredible wealth, and a position of enormous power among the greatest leaders of his adopted land.

Chapter

1

SLUM DOG

R obert Morris, Jr., was born in 1734 in the slime that saturated Liverpool's slums. Indeed, the very name "Liverpool" referred to Mersey River *mud*, or (in old English) *lieur*, that *pooled* on streets in heavy rains, oozing into every entryway, courtyard, and ground-level dwelling. The mix of mud and sewerage fouled the air with an odor that alerted sailors at sea that they were approaching Liverpool.

By 1734, though, the little English town had modernized some of its waterfront and metamorphosed from a backwater of barely 5,000 to a bustling port of almost 20,000. Its magnificent New Dock—the world's first commercial wet-dock—had replaced an obsolete inland port up the Mersey River estuary, where decades of accumulating silt had clogged the river with mud and made the old port unusable and much of the town uninhabitable.

A 3 ½-acre showpiece six years in the building, New Dock commanded a breathtaking view of the Irish Sea, accommodated as many as 100 square riggers at a time, and drained Mersey River waters—and some of its mud—into the sea during heavy rains.

"There is no town in England, London excepted, that can equal Liverpool for the fineness of the streets [and] the beauty of the buildings," English author Daniel Defoe chortled after touring the new part of Liverpool after New Dock opened. "Many of the houses are all of stone and the rest of brick."[1]

Hidden by the brick and stone houses that awed Defoe, however, lay an array of ugly "courts"—three- and four-sided housing complexes built around courtyards all but covered by with mud-encrusted filth and raw sewerage.

Robert Morris was born in one of those courts.

To the pride of most Liverpudlians, New Dock propelled Liverpool past Bristol and London as England's "undisputed slaving capital" and "by far the largest slave port in the Atlantic world."[2] In the decade ended in 1760, some 500 slave ships had sailed in and out of New Dock.

They accounted for 56 percent of all British slavers plying the "the middle passage" of the "triangular trade" that fueled fields of the

A Liverpool court where Morris spent his boyhood..

American South and British Caribbean islands with the blood and sweat of slaves.[3]

"Liverpool has an opulent, flourishing and increasing trade to Virginia and the English colonies in America," the author of *Robinson Crusoe* boasted, without mentioning the slave trade. "They...send ships to Norway, to Hamburg, and to the Baltic, as also to Holland and Flanders; so they are...universal merchants."[4]

Although abolitionism had gained some traction in England as Robert Morris was growing up, there were still nearly 20,000 slaves in the United Kingdom, with most of them in London and northern Scotland, and smaller but noticeable numbers in port towns like Liverpool.

In addition to its reputation as England's slaving capital, Liverpool gained fame for high rates of theft, prostitution, and juvenile crime. In building the landings for multi-masted sailing ships, planners of New Dock had failed to build enough warehouses for cargoes. Although New Dock proved one of the wonders of the maritime world, most piers lay open, unprotected by enclosures and sparsely guarded—a veritable feeding trough for thieves, with sugar, coffee, spices, rice, and other foodstuffs there for the taking after nightfall. Midnight darkness also cloaked gangs who plundered ships for more valuable cargoes—rum, tobacco, bags of rice or beans, even bales of cotton and sailors' clothing—anything looters could find and carry off.

Author/mariner Herman Melville would later describe the Liverpool docks as "putrid with vice and crime to which perhaps the round globe does not furnish a parallel...haunts in which cursing, gambling, pick-pocketing, and common iniquities are virtues." [5]

As crowds massed on New Dock by day to watch tall sailing ships enter and leave the inner pool, swarms of dexterous urchins like Morris darted between gawkers, harvesting watches, purses, jewelry, coins, and sundry souvenirs from men's pockets and women's handbags.

Like Morris, most of Liverpool's urchins had emerged from long lines of anonymous mariners of unknown ranks. One of his mariner grandfathers, Andrew Morris, made extra money snatching trinkets in foreign ports to sell in Liverpool, where he housed his wives and children in a slum by the Mersey River—a mariners' district similar to those of most port cities then. Although the British recognized mariners at sea as essential to the nation's defense in war and its trade and prosperity in peace, they shunned them and their kin for being too different from land-based society to live beside them.

Novelist Henry Fielding blackened mariners as having been "discharged from the common bonds of humanity" when they reached land. They "glory in the languages and behavior of savages."[6]

Daniel Defoe, a mariner himself once, was equally uncharitable, charging sea dogs on shore with becoming "violent fellows...[who] swear violently, whore violently, drink punch violently, and spend their money when they have it violently."[7]

Nothing else is known about Andrew Morris or his wife Maudlin except for one son, Robert Morris—the first in the family known to bear that name. He apparently eschewed the sea in favor of on-shore service at Foster, Cunliffe & Sons, one of Liverpool's larger traders.

Like most Liverpool slum dogs, the elder Morris talked maritime talk, swearing, drinking, and whoring like a mariner, but gaining some standing as a trader. By 1738, he had sired at least nine children by almost as many ladies and faced such intense pressures to provide for his progeny and their mums that he fled to the anonymity of British America. Before shipping out, however, he left one bequest for the oldest of the brood he left behind: his name. Thus, one of his children evolved from "Boy" to Robert Morris, Jr.

Within weeks after Robert Morris, Sr., had left Britain, Robert, Jr.'s mother abandoned her son to the care of an elderly lady who may or may not have been his grandmother. He never saw his mother again and lived the rest of his childhood with the old lady in a mariner slum, where "surface water and fluid refuse of every kind stagnate in the street," according to Dr. William Duncan, Britain's first Medical Officer of Health.

Especially in hot weather, he said, "the more solid filth" created a "pestilential influence." Without toilets, sewers or underground drains, the only means for carrying off fluid dirt was "a narrow, open, shallow gutter...but even this is very generally choked up with stagnant filth."

Duncan discovered as many as forty people living in the cellars of some courts and an infant mortality rate of fifty percent.[8]

No records describe how Robert Morris, Jr., survived so bleak a childhood—or how he learned to read, write, and do simple arithmetic, but learn he did.

Hunger, though, forced most slum pups like Morris to steal from nearby food stalls or from open crates on the waterfront. As they acquired advanced digital skills, they bounced through crowds on the piers, slipping their tiny hands in and out of pockets and handbags, then darting away. Some with less larcenous instincts earned pennies making nails—a common trade among children then. A few swept floors in the warehouses along the docks, again, for a penny or two for hours of brutal work and abuse.

Liverpool's "New Dock," the world's first commercial "wet dock," in 1750.

In America, meanwhile, Robert Morris, Sr., had transformed the relatively small Oxford, Maryland, outpost of his English trading firm into a successful tobacco exporter.[9]

Oxford had been a sleepy little port, when Morris, Sr., arrived in 1738, and, like many such outposts, it offered many settlers with checkered pasts an ideal opportunity to reinvent themselves. Robert

Morris, Sr., did just that, becoming one of the town's more productive merchants, expanding his company's store and helping Oxford itself grow. He bought one of the town's better homes. Then, intent on matching the dynastic status of established merchants whose store-fronts displayed "& Son" after their names, he renamed his shop Robert Morris & Son.

As an afterthought, he sent for Robert Morris, Jr.

But the relationship implied by the store's new name never developed between Robert Morris & Son. The two had not known each other as the boy grew up in Liverpool—and they did not get along after the boy arrived in Oxford. Robert Morris, Sr., had bettered himself in many ways, but he still whored, and, not long after his son arrived, his paramour gave birth to a daughter.

Robert Morris, Jr., by then a demanding adolescent, became an unwanted, added responsibility. Robert Morris, Sr., decided to rid himself of "& Son" by signing a seven-year contract that would force the boy to work as an indentured apprentice at a Philadelphia trading firm.

Young Morris, however, was fortunate to find himself bound to a firm whose English-born owner, Charles Willing, offered apprentices opportunities to grow with the firm by learning skilled trades from the firm's master craftsmen. It was an opportunity for which Robert Morris, Jr., would remain deeply grateful throughout his life.

At the time, most apprenticeships proved little better than bondage, replete with harsh living conditions, beatings, deprivation, and tasks that had less to do with learning a craft than performing unskilled slave labor. So many apprentices fled their masters that adults, eager for rewards, routinely collared unaccompanied children on streets and dragged them screaming to jail, where the youngsters remained until they could prove their identities.

Nestled among sixty piers on Philadelphia's bustling Delaware River waterfront, Willing & Company operated a retail store, warehouse, counting house, and a wharf where the company's three square-riggers sailed in and out carrying, among other things, American wheat and tobacco to Europe and returning to Philadelphia with wines and a few passengers—usually indentured servants and apprentices.One ship plied the "middle passage" on the triangular trade route carrying African slaves to America. "Just imported from the Coast of Africa," the company's advertisement proclaimed in a Philadelphia newspaper:

> "One Hundred and Seventy five Gold Coast Negroes. In the West India Islands, those of the Gold Coast are in much greater esteem and higher valued than any others on Account of their natural good Dispositions, and being better capable of hard Labour."[10]

Willing abandoned the slave trade, however, when high mortality rates at sea reduced the number of slaves who survived the trip to unprofitably low levels.

From the outset, young Morris proved himself an indefatigable worker—at menial chores at first, then, as he grew bigger and stronger, stepping onto the wharf to help load and offload shiploads of crates and barrels and roll them in and out of the warehouse.

When Morris turned 16, though, his father died in a freak accident disembarking from a ship in Oxford harbor. Alienated from his son in life, he nonetheless left Robert, Jr., about £2,500 and "all the rest and residue of my goods, chattels, merchandise, apparel, and personal estate whatsoever." Although the bequest came with some conditions, it proved enough to give the boy considerable financial independence.

Robert Morris, Sr., had also left some money to his paramour and £100 each for her daughter (most likely his) and for the child with whom she was still pregnant (most certainly his) when he died. Robert Morris, Jr., soon had a baby half-brother—Thomas Morris—for whom his father's will designated Robert, Jr., surrogate father. Although Robert enjoyed and, indeed, doted over the infant and assumed as many of the responsibilities of a father as he could, Thomas would soon emerge an incorrigibly malevolent young man and constant threat to his older half-brother's career and family.

Still an apprentice when Thomas Morris was born, Robert Morris, Jr., could have used his inheritance to buy out his apprenticeship bond. He could then quit the piers free and unencumbered, with enough cash to rent living quarters and open a small trading firm of his own.

Clearly gifted with an ear for languages, he had learned the jargon, if not the refinements of French, Spanish, German, and Dutch on the docks of Liverpool and Philadelphia. He had also developed an astonishing command of mathematics and calculating skills, along with the basic tricks of trading.

He accidentally put his skills to work the first time after overhearing a Dutch dockworker mention a stunning increase in orders for flour from Holland. With Charles Willing bedridden with yellow fever, Morris posed as the company's substitute trader and bought as much flour as he could, risking company funds as well as his own inheritance.

When a ship arrived from Flanders a few days later with a stack of orders for flour and word of a full-scale European flour shortage, Philadelphia flour prices soared. Morris sold all the flour he had bought, doubling his own and the company's money—without seeing or even smelling the flour he had bought and sold. Robert Morris had taken his first steps towards becoming America's first great capitalist.

Sensing the boy's gifts, owner Charles Willing added to Morris's rewards by making the training of his gifted young apprentice a personal priority. Though still bonded with several years remaining in his apprenticeship, Morris felt free for the first time in his life—truly happy and revering his employer and mentor.

Willing, in turn, gave the young man responsibilities in the counting house, teaching him to keep accounts and track names and values of foreign currencies. The youngster's quick mind learned to convert currencies instantly, honing all the mental and mathematical tools of seasoned merchant-traders. He also met and befriended the owner's son Thomas Willing.

Three years older than Morris, young Willing had returned from England in 1750 after four years acquiring a classical English education at an Anglican academy in Bath. He then spent a year at London's Inner Temple at the Inns of Court, where he learned British law before going to live with a wealthy uncle for a year. His uncle introduced his nephew into London society, and the young man returned to America in 1749 with all the education and social skills of a perfect British gentleman.

Once in Philadelphia, he began working for his father, who changed the company name to Charles Willing & Son and put his son in the counting house with Morris to learn the business.

Schooled exclusively among England's social elite, young Willing lacked the quick mind and sharp tongue of rough-hewn traders who peopled trading firms along Philadelphia's waterfront. Willing and Morris became immediate friends, however, with each feeding off the other's knowledge and skills and sharply different perspectives of the world. Morris, moreover, was eager to return Charles Willing's favors by mentoring the son.

By then, Robert Morris, Jr., had accumulated and read enough books to improve his knowledge, speech, dress, and demeanor. In doing so, he developed an insatiable thirst for wealth and its accoutrements. He listened in rapt attention to Willing's vocabulary, intonations, gestures, and "gentlemanly" facial expressions, and he absorbed Willing's every description of life in London's elegant Mayfair.

While careful never to reveal his own history as a slum dog on Liverpool's docks, Morris tutored Willing in the intricacies of commodities pricing and trading, and futures trading, while trying his best to absorb Willing's gentlemanly ways and demeanor, including his dress, his rich vocabulary, his intonation and pronunciation, his restrained gestures and laughter, his expressions and responses. Morris had already developed chameleonic skills that allowed him to blend into any and every segment of Philadelphia society, and he used his skill wisely. He seemed to find something new and interesting in everyone he met and soon integrated into every segment of society he frequented.

As he learned social skills from Willing, Morris introduced his employer's son to the mysteries of trading and its variations. He taught his friend such trading practices as arbitrage, which enriched a few traders and bankrupted almost everyone else who dared buy and sell the same commodities in different markets to try to profit from the "spread," or price differences.

He showed Willing how the same tactics used to amass profits in commodities markets often applied in money markets, where one could lend borrowed money at higher interest rates than the rates paid to borrow those funds—borrowing at six percent, for example, and relending the same funds for eight, ten, even twelve percent. All depended on market demand and the differences in different markets of the world.

Morris amazed Willing with his skills, daring, and remarkably consistent success. The two formed a close friendship as well as business relationship that would last their entire lives.

In 1754, Charles Willing died, leaving his firm, his fortune, and his family to his son Thomas. Along with responsibilities for running an important business, however, young Willing now had to care for his widowed mother and eight younger brothers and sisters, all minors. The City Council added to Willing's burdens by appointing him to his father's Council seat. In addition, the Council named him secretary to Benjamin Franklin's Pennsylvania delegation at the heralded "Albany Congress," the New World's first such intercontinental gathering,

The Congress was to bring representatives from every English-speaking North American colony together for the first time and, in effect, presage their eventual union as a single nation. Set to convene from June 18 to July 11, 1754, the Congress would force Willing to leave Philadelphia and entrust oversight of his family, his business, and all his personal affairs to his friend Robert Morris. It was a pivotal moment in the lives of both young men.

For Willing, the Albany Congress offered a chance to become an intimate of the great Franklin and other luminaries and help decide the fate of a continent. For Morris, it would offer his first chance to lead a great and growing enterprise by himself in the most important city of the New World. Each accepted the challenge eagerly.

The Albany Congress proved historic—less for what it did than what it didn't do. British authorities had called on representatives of Connecticut, Maryland, Massachusetts, New Hampshire, New York, Pennsylvania, and Rhode Island to write a treaty of peace with hostile Native American tribes along Lake Erie and the Ohio River Valley.

Franklin, however, extended the scope of the proceedings by proposing a "Plan of Union" to unite American colonies in a new, semi-independent quasi-nation led by a president-general, appointed (and paid) by the crown. A "Grand Council" elected by the colonial assemblies and independent of Britain's Parliament would assume Parliament's legislative authority and write all Union laws, subject to veto by only the president-general and the crown.

Stunned yet thrilled by Franklin's audacity, young Willing and the other delegates roared their approval—only to find on returning home that colonial legislatures and Britain's government had rejected Franklin's proposal out of hand.

In Philadelphia, meanwhile, Willing's absence had left Morris as sole manager of Willing & Co. He met every ship, supervised loading and unloading each of them. He worked with buyers, suppliers, and traders, bid for cargoes on other ships, worked through the night and into early morning recording each day's transactions. His hunger for added revenues was insatiable.

Knowing from first-hand experience that disgruntled dockworkers often sabotaged cargoes, Morris made a point of getting to know his workers individually, praise them, slip them extra money for jobs well done. He instructed nearby tavern keepers to buy each of his workers a last pint before he left for the night—and bill him, Robert Morris, for the brew.

In turn, the men embraced him. He spoke their language, understood theirs. They reported every rumor from incoming ships and on the docks. *Hamburg was short* on this commodity; *Lisbon long* on that one; a Liverpool buyer had outbid a London trader for another.

Morris responded instantly, tipping for the tip, then buying what Hamburg traders needed most, selling what Lisbon held in excess, and redirecting to Liverpool shipments that had been destined for London. To buy whatever cargoes he needed, he ignored his cash balances and issued certificates of foreign exchange—essentially checks for foreign currencies drawn on overseas banks.

Although he seldom had specie, or hard money, to back up the certificates he issued, he knew that weeks—even months—would pass before his kited paper could cross the ocean for collection. In the interim, he sold enough commodities to cover costs of earlier purchases and mastered, as few others did, the art of juggling sales and payments, while keeping them balanced and yielding constant profits to the juggler. He mastered the art of doing business—buying and selling huge inventories—without spending a penny.

When Willing returned to Philadelphia, Franklin kept him busy for days compiling, transcribing, and seeing to the printing of notes from the Albany Congress. When he finally found time to visit the counting house, the growth in revenues amazed him, but the filth of the waterfront and dark dismal atmosphere of the offices left him less than eager to resume working at the firm.

He had mixed with high government officials, debated policies to shape a continent; he prided his elegant clothes, savored fine wines, and enjoyed exchanging graceful phrases that enhanced the political life of the city, colony, and British Empire. The Albany Congress had left him addicted to political theater. Thomas Willing now looked forward to filling his late father's seat on the Philadelphia City Council—and never again looking at, let alone counting, hogsheads on the waterfront.

In any case, Robert Morris had become the heart and soul of Willing & Co. So Thomas Willing asked his friend to assume daily management of the firm as managing partner, and, in 1754, he changed the name of the company to Willing Morris & Company.

A partnership in the trading world did not necessarily mean a fifty-fifty split of assets or net profits, however. It simply meant a pooling of common physical assets and a pledge not to compete with each other for new clients. Partners shared costs and use of such common facilities as warehouses, cargo ships, transport wagons, and partners agreed to act as one in trading with new clients, but each retained all profits derived from those clients that were his before the merger and any new clients he developed on his own .

Thus, when Willing invited Morris to join the firm as a partner, Morris only accounted for about one-fourth of the firm's income, while the accounts Willing had inherited from his father provided 75 percent of the firm's income. Although Willing's income began falling, Morris proved a loyal friend, seeing to the maintenance and even the growth of his partner's income as the firm expanded.

And expand it he did—spectacularly. Morris added more ships, widening the reach and nature of company trading operations. In addition, he developed a new method of financing expansion by printing and selling securities tied to individual ships or trades, thus limiting company liability.

Facing a scarcity of gold, silver, and currency backed by gold or silver, Morris coaxed a group of equally large trading firms to issue a series of combined promissory notes yielding five percent interest annually. In effect the equivalent of today's corporate bonds, the promissory notes produced a stream of cash lured from the hiding places of hoarders into the Willing Morris cash drawer to underwrite the company's trading operations.

As Willing Morris grew, Morris pressed for even more growth, soliciting smaller or less prosperous trading firms to let Willing Morris act as their agent in Philadelphia and elsewhere around the globe, buying and selling anything and everything and collecting commissions on each transaction.

As his firm handled more and more merchandise, Morris expanded the company fleet to carry more goods to and from foreign ports, paying on average, £1,000 for a two-deck cargo ship that he could resell for at least £700 two years later after having made six to ten round trip voyages and selling twelve to twenty shiploads of cargo.

To hedge against losses from storm damage, shipwrecks, spoilage, and piracy, Morris was shrewd enough to sell "paper" with a promise of a share in the profits from the sale of each cargo that arrived safely. Investors would lose all if the cargo failed to arrive at its destination intact, but Morris would keep their investments.

Morris, in effect, was ostensibly gambling, but invariably winning on bets he had fixed in advance. Although it claimed his share of victims, Morris-style capitalism proved far more humane than mercantilism, which relied heavily on serfdom and slave labor and claimed the lives of whole armies to enrich a small ruling class.

The capitalism that Morris developed enriched him and his family and friends, of course, but it also enriched partners, suppliers, customers, a range of financial middlemen, hundreds, even thousands, of workers Morris employed. Eventually, he enriched the entire American nation.

As the firm and its fortunes thrived under Morris's guidance, Willing embraced public life, accepting appointment as a trustee of the University of Pennsylvania, then winning appointment as mayor of Philadelphia, the most important city of the Americas.[11] Morris, meanwhile, leaped to the summit of the city's business community, shedding almost all traces of his former existence as a Liverpool slum dog.

Willing did not cease to make occasional appearances at the firm, of course, and friendship alone sufficed to bring him into frequent contact with Morris.

In addition, Morris insisted on meeting regularly to keep his partner informed about the firm's activities and progress. Well aware of the thieves and scoundrels who peopled the trading world, Morris believed a foundation of mutual trust between him and his partner was the only certain way of ensuring the firm's continued growth and success.

At one meeting, Willing elated Morris with an imaginative proposal to call on Philadelphia's leading merchants—all of them competitors—to pool up to £100,000 pounds each in a fund to insure member losses from Indian raids on land and pirate and privateer attacks at sea. The big traders agreed enthusiastically and created so large a fund that it not only protected its original participants against losses, it allowed Morris to sell marine insurance to trading firms that had not contributed to the original capital pool. Suddenly, Willing Morris & Co. was in the cargo insurance business and on its way to becoming America's first conglomerate corporation.

But then the trading world changed dramatically.

In the early 1750s, French settlers from Canada and British settlers from the Atlantic provinces had been moving in ever greater numbers into the fertile Ohio River Valley wilderness. Inevitably, conflicting claims and counterclaims produced bitter disputes over lands that both Britain and France claimed as their own. By 1754, French troops had moved southward to bolster claims of their countrymen, even building forts to defend against possible British retaliation.

In 1754, the governor of Britain's Virginia colony sent militia colonel George Washington with a band of troops to warn the French to withdraw from lands that Virginia settlers had claimed. Spotting a force of about fifty French troops encamped for the night in western Pennsylvania, Washington ordered his men to ambush the French, firing the first shot himself.

The slaughter "only lasted a quarter of an hour before the enemy was routed," Washington wrote to his adoring eighteen-year-old brother Augustine. "We killed the Commander...as also nine others....Indians scalped the dead and took part of their arms."[12]

Although Washington hoped his assault would prove decisive in determining sovereignty over the West, it ignited the flames of what became the world's first world war—a brutal multi-national war that would last seven years, spread across eastern Canada and the Atlantic Ocean into western Europe, Africa, even India.

By 1756, the Anglo-French war had reached global proportions. Austria, Saxony, Sweden, Russia, and, later, Spain—each lusting for colonies in the Americas—joined France, while Hanover, whose princes had acceded to the British throne in 1714, jumped into the fray with its ally Prussia to support the English.

As war turned the seas more treacherous for trade, cargo vessels armed themselves, with some ships carrying as many as one hundred guns and disguising themselves as warships.

Robert Morris had little choice but to add armed vessels to his cargo fleet—usually English brigs with 24, 30 or 44 guns, most often six pounders (i.e., firing six-pound cannonballs) but often heavier and more destructive. Although he chartered at least one 74-gun ship, the number of guns on any ship was meaningless if the ship did not have the necessary complement of skilled men to work the guns and if the range of cannon fire was too small to inflict damage on a far-off hostile vessel.

Although Thomas Willing distanced himself from day-to-day operations on the piers, he nonetheless stayed in daily contact with Robert Morris—during extended mid-day dinners at the popular City Tavern or in tête-à-têtes in his study or library at the Willing mansion. Philadelphia was a relatively small city then. Although America's largest and richest city, it stretched barely three miles in one direction and two in the other. It was difficult indeed to miss seeing one's friends and relatives at least once on one's daily rounds.

In one such encounter, Willing noted that the larger ships Morris had added to the fleet had increased the size and value of many company shipments. He urged Morris to accompany the most valuable of these as a "supercargo,"[13] or cargo master—i.e., a company representative who sailed aboard a ship with his company's cargoes, directly overseeing their uploading, downloading, purchase, and sale.

Although smaller trading companies routinely commissioned ship captains or first mates to oversee sales of their cargoes in foreign ports, companies with substantially larger or more valuable cargoes often sent their own, more experienced (and trusted) traders with shipments as "cargo masters," to watch over their property and extract better prices.

Willing agreed to return to the counting house temporarily while Morris set off just such a mission on the high seas. By then, Morris had hired a skilled foreman to supervise the piers and an equally gifted chief clerk in the counting house. Although Morris knew Willing would have little to do in the way of supervision, his presence as partner would lend authority to the orders of the foreman and chief clerk in the absence of Morris.

With the Anglo-French war raging in Canada and the high seas, Morris did not relish an ocean voyage, but late summer of 1759 saw a surprise attack by British troops on Quebec and French surrender of the town and the entire province. Not long after, the French ceded all Canada and the surrounding North Atlantic waters to England.

In late summer, as Morris boarded a company galleon for his first adventure as cargo master, Thomas Willing came to the pier to wish his partner a safe voyage and an equally safe return to Philadelphia, where, he promised, "My house shall be your home and myself your friend."[14]

As Morris entered his twenty-seventh year in the spring of 1761, much of the Atlantic grew safe enough to risk transporting goods to and from Britain and many of the islands in the West Indies. To make his voyage as pleasant as possible, Morris saw to it that the interior of the ship on which he was to travel was refurbished to ensure him maximum comfort—in effect mirroring the comforts of the captain's quarters.

For Morris—still a young man after all—sailing off to foreign lands as a cargo master was a heady experience and responsibility. He fulfilled it magnificently—beyond his own expectations. His first trip took him to French spice-island ports on and about Granada; a second trip took him to Britain's nearby sugar islands; and a third into Havana, Kingston, and Port-au-Prince.

At each stop, he bounded onto the pier and haggled like traders twice his age, parroting the demeanor and slang he had learned at Liverpool's New Dock and on Philadelphia piers. Whatever prices dockside buyers bid for his cargo, Morris demanded more, rejecting offers he deemed too low—even when bids were higher than he had anticipated.

To replace cargoes he sold and filled his hold for the return trip—Morris transformed himself into a nonchalant buyer, looking bored as he turned his back and walked away from first offers, scorning prices he deemed too high. Indeed, he deemed every asking price too high, forcing sellers to chase after him, lowering prices as they ran, begging him to make an offer—any offer!

But Morris had an other-worldly knowledge of market values for every product at every port he visited. Blessed with an astounding memory and an ability to make instant, accurate calculations, he was a naturally gifted trader, bellowing prices in British pounds, French livres, Dutch florins, and a dozen other currencies with equal fluency, converting one into another without pausing.

His distinctive voice carried across the waterfront as he barked a mixture of mariner slang, trader slang, British and French—even Dutch—slang, pointing to one bidder or seller, then another, then looking at the sky in exasperation, spinning around, stomping his foot, jumping about like an acrobatic street performer. Puzzled onlookers stared in amazement and amusement, and traders quickly learned not to try outsmarting him. He knew instinctively when to buy, sell, or walk away; he sensed instantly how badly a buyer or seller needed to buy or sell; he intuited impending market shortages or surpluses and took full advantage.

He was brilliant!

As fierce as he was in pier-side bargaining melees, he took pains after the bidding ended to establish warm friendships with key buyers, sellers, and factors, soothing their feelings as he led them arm-in-arm into the nearest tavern to buy drinks—solacing those whose bids he had rejected as well as those with whom he had done business. A round or two often established relationships that spurred his firm's expansion and wealth and filled his pockets and those of his new trading partners with riches.

As it was, Thomas Willing's father Charles had established ties to trading firms in Lisbon, Madrid, Jamaica, Barbados, and Antigua—and of course London, where Charles Willing's brother—Thomas Willing's uncle—headed a trading firm. Morris expanded the number of such "correspondent firms" on his voyages, convincing each potential correspondent to serve as a Willing Morris & Company resident buyer, seller, and banker.

As with traders in England at the time, each would grant Willing Morris ledger credits for goods sold, apply those credits to Willing

Morris purchases, and, in effect, become a branch of Willing Morris in his part of the world.

Each merchant in the global complex agreed to grant Morris credit *without interest* for a year or more and charge no more than five percent interest a year thereafter—and often less. In effect, the cumulative ledger credits he amassed represented a pool of capital which he could invest in long-term capital projects—ship construction, for example.

Without spending a penny of his firm's capital, Morris planted the seeds of modern capitalism, giving corresponding firms overseas entry into the valuable American market while he gained entry into their markets—all, via ledger credits.

Morris went a step further with a selected few, forming formal partnerships with those he deemed trustworthy enough to participate in particularly large investments.

In a few cases when the owner of a prospective partner firm balked at establishing a link with Morris, he staged an unfriendly "leveraged buyout," borrowing enough money to make his offer irresistibly rich, then bleeding the acquired firm's profits for enough money to repay the loan that financed the acquisition.

In the end, Morris formed a global network of Willing Morris & Company franchises, partnerships, lenders, and bankers with a wide enough range of imports and exports to cushion effects of price drops in any market or product or category of products and losses at sea. The network allowed Morris to introduce a variety of trading devices—some of them variations of age old techniques, some of his own invention, often a century or more before they came into common use.

Morris was a master of arbitrage, for example, taking advantage of differences in currency values or commodity prices in different markets, simultaneously buying and selling the same commodity or currency in one market and profiting from the difference or "spread" in another. In some instances, he bought and sold the same shipload of commodities several times as it sailed the seas between its port of origin and its destination, all the time increasing the amount of capital for the multiple transactions.

Morris also traded futures contracts, agreeing in advance to buy or sell commodities at specific prices long in advance of delivery—gambling that market prices would rise or fall by the time he took delivery and allow him to resell all or part of his purchases at a profit.

Far different from today's futures trading, Morris had to buy and sell at a time when trans-Atlantic communications and shipments routinely required four to six weeks or more—if privateers or pirates did not intercept them. Morris often sold commodities he didn't own—so-called phantom trades—months before actually buying and paying for them, but his activities always added to Willing Morris revenues, profits, and *capital*.

As he allowed others to participate in such ventures, the firm became the center of a futures trading market and banking operation, with Willing Morris reaping commissions from every transaction, making it the most important trading firm in America's most important city.

Morris placed few limits on the variety of cargoes his firm bought, sold, or traded. As noted in the advertisement in the Pennsylvania Journal of September 29, 1763, "The goods on hand...will be sold very cheap for ready money or short credit:

> Jamaica spirit [rum] and good assortment of Madeira wines...near three years old, and Tenerife wines, Rhenish wine in casks, Bristol Beer, very good bohea tea in whole and half chests, prunes in hogsheads, boxes of brimstones, boxes of painted and plain glassware, cases of toys, violins, spinning wheels, cordage, two anchors of 12 ct. and 15 ct. wt., Spanish musquets [sic], English ditto powder, an invoice of castor and felt hatts [sic], English ditto tower powder, a large quantity of spermaceti candles, best Havannah [sic] white sugars; a quantity of juniper berries; and aniseeds, with sundry other goods.[15]

Willing Morris ships also carried living cargoes:

Just arrived from Bristol, the ship Sarah...having on board thirty indentured servant men and boys, aged from 16 to 17 years, who have to serve from four to seven years, and amongst them are the following trades and occupations: One white-smith, one black-smith, one lock-smith, one bright-smith, one wool comber, one butcher, one Limeburner, one plasterer [sic] one coachman, one joiner, one brazier, one leather dresser, one mason, one gentleman's servant, one sawyer and the remmainer (sic!) shoemakers, weavers, husbandmen, and labourers. They are to be seen on board said ship, at Willing and Morris's wharf, who have to dispose of their times and can shew the character each servant bore in his own country.[16]

As unused cash and credits accumulated, Morris added other profit-making opportunities such as short-hop, island-to-island trading in the West Indies, short-hop transportation contracts, and real estate. He bought some undeveloped fields on West Indian sugar islands, land on the American Gulf Coast, a failed plantation in Mississippi to develop orange groves, and he bought unsettled lands

in western Pennsylvania, that he divided into parcels for resale to prospective farmers from the Northeast.

At the time thousands of young men were streaming westward from Massachusetts and Connecticut, where farms were too small to divide among multiple sons and remain viable. Under the custom of primogeniture, the oldest son inherited a farmer's property, forcing younger brothers to look elsewhere for lands of their own to farm. Morris sent agents to find and buy lands in the western Pennsylvania wilderness to accommodate them.

When Morris returned to Philadelphia after one venture as cargo master, his partner Thomas Willing proved himself true to his word by making "my house...your home and myself your friend" and introducing Morris into Philadelphia's exclusive Anglican society—a once-unimaginable social triumph for a Liverpool slum dog.

Although Morris now cavorted like a polished gentleman in Philadelphia's mansions, he harbored a hearty appetite for sex—inherited, perhaps, from his father. To avoid embarrassing his business partner, he assuaged his appetite as discreetly as possible, but grew careless at least once, siring an illegitimate daughter he named Mary, who soon acquired the nickname Polly.

Although Philadelphia was America's largest, most cosmopolitan city, it was too small to hide his assignation (or that of any other major figure, for that matter), but Philadelphia society, high and low, apparently took such events as part of nature's course. Morris provided handsomely for both Polly and her mother, paying for their lodgings and living expenses—and Polly's education. Polly would marry in a quiet ceremony when she turned eighteen. She remained as close as possible to Morris for years thereafter, though never intruding in his public life or his life in society or with his legitimate family.

Polly's birth, however, came at a particularly bad time for Morris; his illegitimate half-brother Thomas had reached adolescence and was demanding favors—and money—and becoming unruly. Morris enrolled the thirteen-year-old in a local academy, promising the boy a job in the Willing Morris counting house if he changed his behavior and did well.

Despite his personal family problems, Morris risked several more ocean voyages as cargo master on Willing Morris ships. On most, he returned triumphant, with extremely profitable cargo sales and purchases that proved equally profitable. He also accumulated lists of new overseas connections that would add still more profits to Willing Morris coffers and turn the enterprise into one of America's largest.

One voyage in the summer of 1761, however, proved disastrous. With the world war at an end in the western hemisphere and the Atlantic, he left Philadelphia expecting to arrive at Liverpool's New Dock in the usual four weeks—five, if storms convulsed the seas. Six weeks passed, however…seven…ten…twelve ….with no word of his or his ship's whereabouts

Ominous rumors spread across Philadelphia's waterfront. No mariners arriving there, or in London, or anywhere else had any news of him or his ship. The British and French navies had had no visual contact with his ship. It had either gone down in a storm, they concluded, and Morris was dead. Or—just as likely and just as cruel a fate—privateers or pirates had captured his ship and condemned crew and passengers to either a swift death or a brutally slow death in captivity as slave laborers.

In either case, dead or alive, Robert Morris had vanished, had been lost at sea, and was probably dead.

Chapter

2

FIREWORKS IN THE SKY

T

he brutal world war—the world's first such multinational conflict—had raged for seven years on five continents and on the oceans in between. America hosted the fiercest fighting from 1756 to 1759, at which time hostilities moved to Europe until 1763, when the two primary combatants, England and France, said they'd had enough and signed the Treaty of Paris ending the war.

When Robert Morris sailed out of Philadelphia at the end of summer in 1761, however, France had already surrendered all of Canada and ceded control of the North Atlantic to British ships. With the Atlantic free of conflict, Morris had ordered a ship full of flour, tobacco, and lumber, the three most common commodities his firm shipped to the West Indies, and he had left for those islands, intending to return with a full load of hogsheads[17] filled with rum.

He left on an "east indiaman," the largest of the late 18th century standard cargo sailing ships. About 175 feet long and more than 40 feet wide, it flew British colors and carried 44 guns, a common number on ships then. To ensure a bit more protection, Morris ordered the ship's exterior painted to resemble a warship.

In January 1762, Spain suddenly entered the war in support of the French to try to prevent Britain from extending her conquest in Canada southward to the Caribbean and into the Gulf of Mexico. Although well armed for a cargo vessel, the Morris ship—like most ships of its kind—lacked skill gunners and could do little to ward off attacks by determined enemy raiders.

Somewhere on its voyage south, a French ship—most likely a privateer—spotted the British colors and captured the Morris ship and its cargo. As with every humiliation in his life, Morris kept details of his and his ship's capture to himself. After missing for months, however, he suddenly and unabashedly materialized, arm in arm with his partner, at the door of the popular City Tavern.

Onlookers gasped in amazement. Although rumors about his possible fate had abounded during his absence, none were based on truth. Only he knew the truth, and he uttered not a word to anyone, not even to his partner and closest friend Thomas Willing. Somehow, Morris had indeed found his way out of captivity to America, but as with details of his life in the Liverpool slums, he remained silent. Even his diaries illuminated none of the dark corners of his personal life. The jolly, outgoing tradesman and bon vivant loved life in America too much to relive even a minute of his miseries elsewhere.

Although mentions of his ordeal have dotted the pages of histories and biographies in the centuries since, none has ever been substantiated. The earliest such report—in 1841—relates his having been "captured by the French and, during a close imprisonment for some time, suffered cruelty of treatment not to be justified by the laws of war nor the usages of civilized nations." In this state of distress, without a shilling, the account goes on, "by exercising his ingenuity, and repairing a watch of a Frenchman, he raised the means of his own liberation and enabled himself to return to Philadelphia to resume the mercantile station from which he had been torn."[18]

The stories of his survival grew even more implausible as time went on. And when he appeared at Philadelphia's popular City Tavern after his captivity, Robert Morris was too rotund and rosy-cheeked—too healthy, with too broad a smile across his face—to reflect any "cruelty of treatment" such as hard labor. Although he knew the rudiments of dockside French, he had never learned watchmaking and is most unlikely to have repaired any Frenchman's watch.

Whatever his ordeal may have been, he somehow managed to extricate himself and return to Philadelphia. He was, after all, a skilled trader and had so mastered the art of selling that admirers believed he could sell George III a new crown.

Into the tavern he now strode, nodding and smiling broadly at each and every attendee, as if he had seen them all the day before. He marched with his partner to their usual table, looking as nonchalant as he knew how while others sat agape.

As whispers filled the air, the two partners exchanged unintelligible whispers of their own. The two headed what had grown into Philadelphia's largest trading firm, and, with Willing deeply involved in the city's political life, most merchants looked to them for leadership in all matters affecting business and the city—indeed, the state—economy.

Despite Morris's silence, partner Thomas Willing had embraced him joyously on his return—as did workers and associates at Willing Morris & Co. All respected his reluctance to discuss his ordeal. He was, after all, the company mastermind who had produced unimaginable wealth for them all. Even the lowest-level employees lived well because of Morris, and all were ecstatic at his safe return.

Thomas Willing hosted several lavish dinners to celebrate his partner's return, which inspired a rush of trading activity at the firm. The British conquest of French and Spanish islands in the West Indies expanded the number of islands flying the British flag and, in turn, the number of islands with which Philadelphia merchants could trade in the West Indies.

Morris reacted quickly, chartering enough ships to accommodate the increased traffic. On average, a shipload of flour to the West Indies, where buyers were at the mercy of sellers, netted profits of 50 percent to 60 percent. The return trip to Philadelphia—with rum and sugar—seldom netted more than 10 percent, but Morris replaced two-way shuttle trade that yielded limited profits on one leg with triangular trade that yielded high profits on all three legs.

Instead of carrying sugar and rum from the Caribbean to America, he sent some ships with sugar and rum to Britain when prices there rose above their levels in America. Once in British ports, his ships then sailed back to America with much-needed manufactured products such as fine furniture, which often yielded extraordinarily high profits in Philadelphia. Except for contractual shipments with specific delivery dates, he eschewed fixed schedules and sent his cargoes wherever prices were highest.

Obviously he could not direct traffic himself in an era before electronic communications. But he recruited a network of loyal "factors" in every port along the American and European coasts and in the West Indies, offering each a secret "partnership" that yielded far more profits than the commissions competitive merchants routinely offered. Morris could, therefore, count on a factor in any and every port to direct or redirect any Morris cargo to the port that would offer the most profitable return.

As other merchants routinely directed their shipments to major ports like London, Morris shipments often sailed into Liverpool or Bristol—so-called "outports," where port charges and transportation costs were lower than in major ports and his local factors, or representatives, could usually obtain higher prices than in major ports such as London. Every Morris factor grew more loyal as he grew richer by helping Morris grow richer.

Adding to the firm's profits were reciprocal corresponding arrangements, with Willing Morris handling imports and exports and associated payments for other firms, much as foreign merchants performed similar services for Willing Morris. International trade functioned on reciprocity, with Morris simply more skilled at profiting from it than most.

Triangular trading schemes had only just helped lift Willing Morris profits to record levels, however, when the British government announced it intended imposing a series of economic measures to force Americans to bear costs of maintaining the British army in America. All but bankrupted by the war with France, Britain suffered further losses when a Native American uprising in the West ended with the destruction of every British post west of Niagara and left the British treasury without funds to spend on defending its North American colonies.

Although the Anglo-French conflict had ended with France ceding most of its North American territory to Britain, the costs of victory for Britain had been higher than the cost of defeat had been for France. Defeat had cost France her North American empire and most of her colonies in Africa, India, and the West Indies, and it had emptied the French national treasury, but it had also left France without the steep costs of governing or defending those possessions.

Victory, with its enormous territorial gains, had transferred those costs to the British, whose treasury was as empty as that of the French. Victory had also swelled Britain's national debt to £130 million (nearly $8 billion today) and added £300,000 in annual costs for military garrisons to protect North American colonists against Native American attacks.

To pay for those garrisons, Parliament raised taxes at home, but the increases put 40,000 Englishmen into debtor's prisons and provoked widespread anti-tax riots. Threatened with a national uprising, Parliament rescinded most of its domestic tax increases and compensated by passing three measures that reflected the sentiment of most Englishmen that Americans should pay costs of their own military protection.

The American Revenue Act raised duties on America's imports and exports, and the Currency Act banned issuance of colonial currency. Parliament also extended the reach of the British Stamp Tax to the colonies. It had been in effect in England for decades and required the purchase and affixment of one or more revenue stamps–often worth less than a penny each—on all legal documents (contracts, wills, deeds, marriage certificates, etc.), newspapers and periodicals, liquor containers, decks of playing cards and a host of other industrial and consumer goods.

Although negligible in its effects on costs of a single item—a newspaper, for example—its cumulative returns were enormous, because it required purchase and attachment of a stamp on each document or product at each stop along its path from producer to consumer—purchase orders at each transfer point, for example, and bills of lading along the multiple routes from producer to consumer.

With Americans scattered over so vast and sparsely settled a continent, London had expected little if any organized popular resistance to the Revenue and Currency Acts or the Stamp Act—certainly nothing generated by a transplanted Englishman from Liverpool's slums.

But in appeasing the English, Parliament provoked the fury of Robert Morris and hundreds of other American merchants. Morris denounced the American Revenue Act as a threat to foreign trade and the Currency Act as a threat to inter-colonial trade. Coming just after a sharp drop in revenues during the Seven Years' War, Morris said, the two acts would end American trade with the West Indies and plunge the colonies into an economic crisis.

"I assert boldly that commerce ought to be free as the air, to place it in the most advantageous state to mankind in general," Morris declared, adding that the interests of merchants and the public "go hand in hand."[19]

In Boston, the city's leading merchant-banker John Hancock seconded Morris. "Times are very bad," Hancock lamented after a number of Boston merchants declared bankruptcy. "Money is extremely scarce and trade very dull."[20]

In passing the American Revenue Act, Parliament raised duties on, and therefore the costs of, almost all American imports not made in Britain or British territories, including coffee, sugar, indigo, wines, and rum. All were central to Willing and Morris volume and profits from trade with the French West Indies.

The second parliamentary measure—the Currency Act—would have all but ended trade in the British West Indies by prohibiting colonies from printing or circulating any currencies that did not originate in Britain.

Although locally printed colonial currency had no monetary value, it served effectively as a medium of colony-wide trade and with the nearby West Indies. Instead of personal IOUs, whose use seldom extended beyond the store or village where its signer was known, handsome paper currency printed by the state and inscribed with the state's name, commanded full face value to buy and sell both in and out of each colony of issue and beyond.

A merchant who might be reluctant to accept a buyer's personal, hand-written I.O.U. generally accepted official-looking notes printed by the state, because he knew his own suppliers would likely do so as well. Given the scarcity of British currency in America, the Currency Act threatened to bring intercolonial trade to a halt.

Philadelphia merchants acted immediately, with Thomas Willing and partner Robert Morris drawing up a petition protesting the new taxes. After they had penned their names at the top, 450 Philadelphia merchants followed suit. In Boston, 250 merchants rallied behind a similar protest, followed by 200 New York merchants. Boston's John Hancock warned his London agent that "the people of this country will never suffer themselves to be made slaves of by a submission to the damned act."[21]

In Philadelphia, meanwhile, Morris and Willing acted to thwart the Currency Act by issuing what they called "promissory notes"—an equivalent of today's corporate notes and bonds. The notes yielded five percent annual interest and, though not currency technically or legally, they temporarily served as a substitute for currency in Philadelphia.

Although British authorities were helpless to drive the corporate notes off the market, small businesses and farmers protested, arguing that Willing Morris could easily drive selected competitors out of business by refusing to redeem notes of some firms and not others. Pennsylvania's colonial Assembly agreed and banned the notes.

To counter the American Revenue Act, Willing Morris did what almost all American traders had done for years: they smuggled. Instead of carrying goods from Europe to British ports before bringing them to America, as required by British law then, Willing Morris ships sailed cargoes of European goods directly to Philadelphia, where local customs officers—all on the unofficial Willing Morris payroll—absented themselves from their customary stations when they spotted a Willing Morris ship coming into port.

Morris also added small, fast sloops to his fleet to sprint in and out of the myriad of small ports and coves along the Atlantic Coast, far from the eyes of British customs officials.

London responded by tightening government controls at sea and on land, but the tighter controls simply provoked more protests.

In mid-1764, Boston merchants ceased importing English leather, lace and ruffles. In Philadelphia, Willing Morris cancelled all existing orders for British goods and organized a merchant boycott of all British imports "until the Stamp Act is repealed." Merchants in Boston and New York joined the boycott.

Infuriated by merchant insolence, Parliament responded by passing a Quartering Act giving troops the right to occupy and live in inns, alehouses, and unoccupied dwellings without warnings or warrants and, in effect, occupy ever major town to put down further Stamp Act protests. The act had the opposite effect.

On the morning of August 14, 1765, a straw effigy of Boston's designated stamp collector–a wealthy Tory merchant—dangled from the limb of an elm tree in the middle of town.

Immediately dubbed the Liberty Tree, it drew an ever-widening crowd, which metamorphosed into a mob that marched to the tax collector's house with the effigy and burned it—then set fire to the house. The royal governor summoned the militia, but the drummers who normally sounded the alarm and most of the militiamen had joined the mob, which marched to the governor's mansion.

One of the architectural jewels of North America, the mansion was a palatial structure crowned by a delicate cupola atop a ring of Ionic pilasters. As the governor fled with his daughter to the protection of British troops in Boston Harbor, the mob broke down the massive doors and, room by room, destroyed everything they could lay their hands on, including the governor's legendary manuscript collection documenting the history of Massachusetts. Rumors swirled through Boston that the mob planned "a War of Plunder, of general levelling & taking away the Distinction of rich & poor."[22]

The Boston rioting set off an epidemic of violence across the colonies, spreading first to Newport, then New York, Philadelphia, and Charleston.

A mob in Newport, Rhode Island, built a gallows for the designated stamp collector, who fled to a British warship in the harbor and promised to resign. Stamp officers elsewhere followed suit, resigning in New Hampshire, Connecticut, New York, New Jersey, Maryland, Virginia, North and South Carolina, Georgia, and even in the Bahamas. In New York City, a mob of about 2,000 marched through the city, and hung effigies of the governor and royal officials on a makeshift gallows.

In Philadelphia, Morris led a mob to the waterfront and prevented a ship carrying stamps from tying up. State Assemblyman John Hughes, the designated Stamp Tax commissioner, feared for his life (with good reason) after protesters hung him in effigy at the State House (now Independence Hall).

As the mob grew in numbers and prepared to find and hang the man himself, Robert Morris tried to calm the mob. As it prepared to set fire to the tax collector's house with its owner inside. Morris and a few others rushed into the house and convinced Hughes to pledge publicly not to sell any of the stamps. He did so, and the mob dispersed.

With Hughes's capitulation, Morris found himself alongside his partner Willing as one of Philadelphia's civic leaders charged by popular demand to do the public's bidding. In January 1766, as the boycott of British imports took hold, merchants appointed him a warden of the port, responsible for spotting violations of the boycott.

It was then that Boston's firebrand lawyer James Otis sent a circular letter to merchants in eleven of the thirteen British colonies urging them to elect delegates to what would become known as the Stamp Act Congress. Delegates, he said, would convene in New York to determine a course of concerted action by all thirteen colonies to obtain repeal of the Stamp Act.

In Pennsylvania's selection process for delegates, however, Quaker reconciliationists led by Philadelphia's John Dickinson outnumbered those favoring any rupture with British authority and elected a delegation opposed to further protests. Left behind in Philadelphia, Robert Morris and his partner were powerless to influence the outcome of the Stamp Act Congress.

After eleven days of deliberation, only six of the nine delegations agreed on and signed a petition addressed to Parliament and to king George III asking for repeal of the Stamp Act.

The petition did not hint at independence, opting instead for an obsequious assertion that colonists "glory in being the subjects of the best of kings.... That we esteem our connection with...Great Britain as one of the great blessings....[and that] subordination to the Parliament is universally acknowledged."[23]

Even the whimper which ended the declaration could not coax a single delegate to risk treason by penning his name on the document. The only signature that appeared was that of the paid clerk.

Although the tone of the petition —or lack of it—outraged Morris and Willing, the boycotts of British products they had helped organize were curtailing trade so much that British merchants staged protests of their own in London against taxing the colonists. Colonial merchants owed them about £4 million, and the flow of orders from America had all but ceased. British exports dropped 14 percent.

With goods piling up inside and outside British warehouses, merchants in London, Bristol, Liverpool, Manchester, Leeds, Glasgow, and other British trading towns inundated Parliament with petitions demanding repeal of the Stamp Act.

In Virginia, George Washington, a major exporter of tobacco, observed, "I fancy the merchants of Great Britain will not be among the last to wish for a repeal."[24]

He proved correct. In mid-January 1766, English merchants warned Parliament that they faced bankruptcy unless normal trade with North America resumed immediately. If Parliament wanted to tax the colonies, they counseled, it should continue the tradition of using indirect hidden taxes such as import duties.

By the end of February 1766, the economic toll in Britain and the demands for repeal grew overwhelming. In March, a year to the day after Parliament had passed the Stamp Act, Parliament repealed it without a single stamp having been affixed to any document or product in America.

In addition, Parliament bowed to merchant demands in the British West Indies to eliminate duties on sugar from Britain's island colonies to mainland America and on molasses from the French West Indies that American distillers used to make rum. Willing Morris trade soon thrived as a result. They added seven more ships and owned shares in so many additional ships that the size of their actual fleet on the high seas was impossible to determine. It was certainly one of if not the world's largest.

Repeal of the Stamp Act was a humiliating defeat for Parliament–particularly because it came at the hands of a constituency without a single vote in either the House of Commons or the House of Lords.

In the end, the British government had collected no new taxes and left its own treasury and many British merchants far poorer than they would have been had it never passed the Stamp Act.

A far more ominous consequence of the act, however, was the appearance of the first organized opposition to parliamentary and royal rule in the colonies–provoked by merchants like Robert Morris and Thomas Willing, who chafed under London's arbitrary regulations and restrictions on free enterprise.

From the arrival of the first British settlers in America, Britain had allowed them to function unfettered by government rules, regulations, or taxes, provided they sold all exports only to Britain or other British colonies. The Stamp Act had been the first British attempt to violate the American free enterprise system, and the rebuff by Morris and other merchants left Parliament incensed at the challenge to its authority.

In mid-May, about a month after the actual vote in Parliament, news of America's success arrived in Philadelphia, New York, Boston, and other ports. There and across the colonies, Americans set aside as a holiday they called "Repeal Day" to celebrate their triumph over the world's most powerful government. Merchants broke open barrels of rum, wine, beer and other beverages for employees, clients, and passers-by to enjoy. Londoners rejoiced as well. The city illuminated its streets, and its merchants—ecstatic over prospects of renewed trade with America–rolled out kegs of wine to serve to dancing celebrants in the lanes outside their doors.

Fireworks lit the sky in Philadelphia, where citizens poured from their homes to dance in the streets. The city's taverns—the London Coffee House, City Tavern, and the like—served free punch and beer. A great parade filled the air with songs and cheers, led by the city's shipwrights who built the ships that made Philadelphia the continent's most important port.

At the State House, Mayor John Lawrence hosted merchants and city leaders at an enormous banquet, where Robert Morris and Thomas Willing toasted each other for their triumph, and Willing embraced his partner as "the man I love most in the world."[25]

It was at one of the great balls that celebrated the Stamp Act victory that Morris first eyed the dazzlingly beautifu, sixteen-year-old Mary White. She turned out to be a daughter of Colonel Thomas and Esther White, the former a distinguished English-born lawyer, a pillar of Philadelphia's Anglican Church, and a founder, with Benjamin Franklin and others, of the Academy and College of Philadelphia (now University of Pennsylvania).

To Robert Morris, fifteen years Mary's senior, she was the epitome of beauty, elegance, erudition, and young womanhood. She was his ideal, as was her family. With her parents and her brother William, a year older than Mary, the Whites were the family Robert Morris had only imagined he might join. They stood at the peak of American society.

Taken by her beauty and her family's stately demeanor, Morris's chameleonic social instinct took hold as he began attending Anglican services each Sunday, learning the liturgy and becoming a practicing Anglican, as he wooed Mary White and her family.

Mary White Morris
(Portrait by Charles Willson Peale, National Portrait Gallery)

As Americans and Englishmen feted the economic recovery that followed repeal of the Stamp Act, bitterness gripped the very souls of the humiliated parliamentarians who had provoked the crisis. Refusing to accept defeat or seek reconciliation, they lit the fuse for the next colonial explosion by passing a "Declaratory Act" on the very day they had repealed the Stamp Act.

Addressing the basic constitutional issue raised by colonists, the act asserted that "the Parliament of Great Britain had, hath and of right ought to have, full power and authority to make laws and statutes of sufficient force and validity to bind the colonies and people of America, Subjects of the Crown of Great Britain in all cases whatsoever."[26]

Those last four unfortunate words—"...in all cases whatsoever"—would eventually cost Britain her empire. In the year that followed, Parliament enacted a series of measures called the Townshend Acts, named for Chancellor of the Exchequer Charles Townshend. The acts ignored American sensibilities against direct taxes by imposing crushing duties on glass, lead, paints, paper, and tea. All but the last were essential elements in home and building construction, while tea was an integral element of the daily American diet and social life.

A second act transferred responsibility for paying colonial governors and judges to the British government. And another Townshend Act called for transporting defendants in the colonies to offshore admiralty courts for trials without juries of their peers.

Infuriated merchants in port cities called for a selective boycott of British goods. "It is surprising to me," wrote Boston's John Hancock in an angry letter to his London supplier, "that so many attempts are made on your side to cramp our trade, new duties every day increasing. In short we are in a fair way of being ruined. We have nothing to do but unite and come under a solemn agreement to stop importing any goods from England."[27]

Virginia's George Washington agreed, complaining to a British merchant , "I think the Parliament of Great Britain hath no more right to put their hands in my pocket, without my consent, than I have to put my hands into yours for money."[28]

In Philadelphia, John Dickinson, the London-educated Quaker lawyer and member of the Pennsylvania Assembly who had drafted the innocuous declaration of the Stamp Act Congress, took a new tack, publishing the first of twelve stirring essays in the *Pennsylvania Chronicle* and *Virginia Gazette*.

Subsequently published by twenty of the twenty-six newspapers in the thirteen colonies, *Letters from a Farmer in Pennsylvania*, as he called his essays, condemned British taxes as unconstitutional and charged Parliament with bleeding the colonial economy.

> If Britain can order us to come to her for necessities...and can order us to pay what taxes she pleases before...we land them here, we are...slaves.... If we can find no relief from this infamous situation...we may bow down our necks, and with

all the stupid serenity of servitude, to any drudgery which our lords and masters shall please to command.[29]

Dickinson's *Letters* convinced Rhode Island and New York to join the spreading boycott. Virginia, New Jersey and Connecticut issued their own petitions, with Virginia also sending a circular letter urging other colonies to support boycott. By the end of 1767, Maryland, Pennsylvania, Delaware, New Hampshire, South Carolina, North Carolina, and New York had each petitioned the king to repeal the Townshend Acts.

Having tasted enough political intrigue during the Stamp Act controversy, Robert Morris decided to remain aloof from the new controversy and focus on keeping the business afloat while Willing seized the political spotlight. Willing enjoyed politics and had already set his eye on the governorship. Morris focused his eye on what he did best: making money.

Refusing to engage Dickinson, Morris used Townshend Act duties as an opportunity make more money—lots of it. Asserting that he was British-born, he declared, "I abhor the Name and Idea of a Rebel. I neither want nor wish a Change of King or Constitution."[30]

A surprising number of Philadelphia merchants followed suit, and, when Thomas Willing called for a meeting of merchants to vote on whether to boycott English imports, fewer than 25 percent of the town's merchants bothered to show up. Like Morris, they were profiting from boycotts in other American ports by importing more British goods.

Morris doubled his company-owned fleet to ten ships, adding or chartering more ships as needed. When necessary, he assumed part ownership of ships whose owners needed injections of capital to assemble crews and set off to sea. In addition to trading commodities and selling marine insurance, Morris & Willing now had a large and expanding stake in the ocean transport business.

Morris profited in other ways as well. Through his network of factors and his ties to merchants and sea captains in ports and cities across Europe and North America, he located the least expensive supplies of the items targeted by the Townshend Act and landed them in Philadelphia at prices that offset the cost of higher duties and allowed him to price them below comparable goods of his competition.

Aware of the possibility that another transatlantic conflict might develop and hurt his transoceanic businesses, Morris acted to diversify his business on land by scooping up cheap land in Pennsylvania farm country and wherever he believed properties would appreciate in value as the nation expanded.

By 1775, Morris boasted that, in addition to capital derived from trade, "we possess valuable landed estates…[and] we are totally free of encumbrances."[31] In effect, he had assembled the world's first conglomerate designed to compensate for revenue declines in one sector of a company's business with revenue increases in other sectors.

Chapter 3
WE LOVE THE PEOPLE OF ENGLAND

A

t sunset on May 9, 1768, John Hancock's small sloop *Liberty* sailed into Boston harbor after crossing the Atlantic from Madeira with a shipload of wine he could easily have smuggled into any number of New England landings. Darkness forced Boston customs inspectors to postpone inspection until morning, at which time they found the ship's hold more than three-quarters empty.

In a dangerously provocative act that forced British retaliation, Hancock had ordered the ship all but emptied during the night, leaving the remaining cargo too small to warrant any duties. A month later, a fifty-gun British man-of-war, the *Romney*, sailed into Boston harbor, its captain thundering to all within earshot,

"The town is a blackguard town and ruled by mobs...and, by the eternal God, I will make their hearts ache before I leave."

As British press gangs swarmed ashore to terrorize the waterfront, a detachment of marines boarded the *Liberty* and tied her fast to a British customs boat and prepared to tow the wine ship away. Before the British ship could do so, however, a mob gathered and pelted the marines with paving stones, then burned the customs boat and beat the customs officials bloody. In the aftermath, British General Thomas Gage ordered ten regiments into Boston "to rescue the Government out of the hands of a trained mob."[7][4]

Although Boston's plight inspired New York merchants to mount another boycott of British goods, Morris and other Philadelphia merchants refused, believing that Hancock himself had purposely and unnecessarily goaded the British to act and that Boston's merchants were provoking British retaliation that threatened the profitable ties of other provinces with the motherland. Morris, for example, smuggled far more wine than Hancock into the American colonies without incident and saw no reason to provoke the British by publicly humiliating them.

In March 1769, Robert Morris married Mary White in the then-Anglican and now Protestant Episcopal Christ Church, whose spire towered over Philadelphia. His bride had turned 19; he was 35. In marrying her after three years a-wooing, Morris joined his partner Thomas Willing and the rest of the Willing family as a full-fledge member of America's aristocracy.

Already one of the city's wealthiest men, Morris bought both a family pew in Christ Church and the mansion of former Governor Richard Penn on Front Street. The mansion stood far enough away from the waterfront to avoid its noises and odors but comfortable close enough for Morris to walk to and from work each day..

Morris hired a staff of servants to ensure his wife's comforts. He doted on her, adored her, listened in disbelief at his good fortune as she spoke, recited poetry, or sang. Nine months after their marriage, she bore their first child, Robert Morris III.

Besides Mary, the Whites had a son William, a year older than Mary and the future presiding bishop of America's Episcopal Church. Mary's father had insisted on educating his daughter as well as his son as they grew up on their father's seven-thousand-acre estate. Of Mary, a poet at Mary's wedding remarked,

> *In lovely White's most pleasing form,*
> *What various graces meet!*
> *How blest with every striking charm!*
> *How languishingly sweet!*[32]

After his wedding, Robert Morris, Jr., further embedded himself in high- Anglican society by purchasing an eighty-acre farm about three miles from Philadelphia and transforming it into a palatial summer estate for Mary. He built an elaborate two-story British manor house on a knoll with a grand view of the beautiful Schuylkill River.

Dubbing his estate "The Hills," Morris embellished his property "in a style and manner unknown in this country," according to Charles Henry Hart, the noted nineteenth century art historian and president of the Pennsylvania Academy of the Fine Arts.

Curved walkways carved through magnificent English gardens past a pond laden with goldfish and flowering lily pads. Morris built a cluster of outbuildings that included a gardener's cottage, a coach house, an ice house, and several heated greenhouses where he raised "all kinds of tropical fruit." The hot houses and ice house were "the first

The Robert Morris country home he dubbed "The Hills."

introduced in America," Hart said.[33] Mary Morris called The Hills "all that's beautiful to the eye.... Nature never appeared so lovely nor promised such a profusion of her gifts."[34]

Mrs. Samuel Breck, the wife of a prominent Philadelphia merchant, described The Hills: as "the pure and unalloyed which the Morrises sought to place before their friends, without the abatements which so frequently accompany the displays of fashionable life. No badly cooked or cold dinners at their tables; no pinched fires upon their hearth; no paucity of waiters; no awkward looms in their drawing rooms."[35]

2. Robert Morris's girth grew in tandem
with his wealth. (Library of Congress)

The Hills also served as a perfect site for entertaining the world's leading merchants and political leaders, extending the reach of Willing Morris trade and influence into governmental affairs.

As an international trader, Morris accumulated one of the finest wine cellars in America and hosted celebrated political and business leaders from Europe as well as North America. As he put it to Virginia's Benjamin Harrison, he made it a "practice of mixing business and pleasure and have ever found them useful to each other."[36]

A visiting French Army general would later describe Morris as "a large man, very simple in his manners; his mind is subtle and acute, a zealous republican and a 'distinguished part in social life and [business] affairs."[37]

—-

As summer ended, and blustery winds combined with an early autumn frost, the British military occupation made the lives of Boston's innocents intolerable.

After Morris had moved back to town for the winter, he and other Philadelphia merchants finally relented about signing the boycott, with Willing signing his name at the top of the list of boycotters and Morris signing lower down.

Deprived of the Philadelphia market, British exports to America immediately collapsed to less than half their normal levels, Parliament had no choice but to capitulate: it repealed all Townshend Act tariffs save one on tea, which, to save face, it left in effect as a symbol of Parliamentary rule over the Americas.

Parliament's concession had little effect on growing unrest in America, however. In Boston, a mob retaliated against the tea tariff by boarding three ships and dumping 342 chests of tea worth about $1 million in 21st century currency into Boston Harbor. To Morris's surprise and shock, rioters in New York and Annapolis staged their own tea parties.

"I am sorry to say there are some of us who cannot bear the thought of reconciliation on any terms," Morris responded. "I cannot help condemning this disposition."[38]

Parliament responded to what the press dubbed the "tea parties" with a chorus of angry shouts and a series of so-called "Coercive Acts" to force Americans to submit to parliamentary rule. One of these, the Boston Port Bill, blocked all trade by land or sea in and out of Boston, including food, until those responsible for the "Boston Tea Party" repaid the East India Company for its lost tea shipments.

It then annulled the right of local self-government in Massachusetts and punished American colonial leaders in all the colonies—including Robert Morris—by passing the Quebec Act. That legislation stripped New York, Pennsylvania, Virginia, Connecticut, and Massachusetts and their citizens of sovereignty and property rights in the West along the Ohio River Valley and attached all those lands to Canada.

In Philadelphia, Robert Morris tried to remain aloof and focus on business, but the Massachusetts provincial assembly responded by declaring independence from Britain. It called on all its citizens to arm themselves and form a state militia, and it called on leaders of the other colonies to meet at an intercolonial Congress to form a united front against Britain.

The action stunned Americans across the colonies. Wherever Morris went—in every tavern, every salon, even on the streets and docks and in his own counting house—every one talked of Boston's plight, the Quebec Act, and the need for concerted action by provincial leaders. Every merchant in Philadelphia asked Morris for guidance. Though far from espousing rebellion, Morris modified his position on reconciliation by conditioning it on the continuation of "undisturbed enjoyment of the freedom we claim...and atom of property."

Always the capitalist and champion of free enterprise, Morris demanded unrestricted free trade, unfettered by government taxes and regulations of any kind and the return of western properties to their rightful owners—including himself.

After an appeal by Boston leaders, fifty-six delegates from twelve colonies streamed into Philadelphia in August 1774 for the first "Constitutional Congress." Like Robert Morris, most Philadelphians welcomed the delegates enthusiastically in hopes they would develop a means of reconciling colonial differences with the motherland and let everyone get back to work and conduct business profitably.

To ensure that the delegates heard their voices, a few Philadelphians leaped into delegate carriages as they entered town to express their views and, in some cases, invite delegates to the nearest tavern or even to their homes.

Although portly Robert Morris did no leaping, he was the quintessential man of business who thrived by entertaining and influencing important men. In the course of the convention, he not only entertained most delegates, he formed warm friendships with New York's John Jay and Virginia's George Washington, both of whom he invited to several dinners at his home in town. He grew particularly close to Washington, whom he invited to spend a weekend at The Hills.

Staunch Quaker reconciliationists, however, had dominated Pennsylvania voting for delegates to Congress, and they ignored both Willing and Morris in favor of lawyer Joseph Galloway.

A brilliant speaker and close friend of Benjamin Franklin, Galloway dominated Congress proceedings by presenting a plan of union between Britain and the American colonies.

Believing that both America and Britain would prosper with such a union, Galloway suggested that the king appoint a president general for life to head the union and serve at the king's pleasure. A grand council of representatives from each colony would handle local legislation, but the president general would have irrevocable veto power over any acts passed.

Congress not only voted down Galloway's plan, it showed its anger by expunging it from the minutes of the Congress.

With Willing and Morris and their closest political allies peppering congressional delegates in nearby taverns and at private dinner parties, the Congress condemned Parliament's Coercive Acts and the Quebec Act as "unjust, cruel, and unconstitutional," and it passed ten resolutions stating colonist rights, among them "life, liberty, and property." Another resolution demanded exclusive legislative powers for the colonies, independent of Parliament, "in all cases of taxation and internal polity" subject only to royal veto.

Congress also pledged to continue colony-wide economic sanctions against British trade until Parliament repealed thirteen acts that the delegates believed violated American rights under the British constitution.

Then, in the most remarkable action, delegates voted to form a Continental Association of American colonies and pledged to end imports from Britain, end the slave trade, and end consumption of products from the entire British Empire until Parliament repealed the Coercive Acts and Quebec Act.

The Association would also ban all exports to Britain, Ireland, and the West Indies. All the American restrictions on trade with Britain were to go into effect on December 1.

Although it had no official status or authority, Congress nonetheless called on "every county, city, and town" in America to elect committees to oversee the sanctions of Congress and expose "all such foes of the rights of British-Americans as "enemies of American liberty."[39]

Despite his objections to any trading restrictions, Philadelphians elected Robert Morris to their committee. They could obviously not exclude the city's most important importer and exporter.

To elevate his importance, they named him chief inspector to determine the national origins of import and exports. Fortunately for both Morris and his company, the embargoes were not to take effect until December 1, which allowed him to take full advantage of the time remaining to engage in unfettered free trade.

Eager to sell as many American goods as possible to Britain and her possessions and to import as many British products as possible, Morris acted quickly. He expanded his fleet to more than fifty ships, adding two 200-ton brigs, each carrying about a dozen six-pounders.

The two brigs were his largest, fastest, and sturdiest. He ordered his fleet to be loaded with more than a year's supply of flour and other American goods and sent them to both England and Lisbon, Portugal, on the shortest routes to Europe.

Hedging against the possibility of war with Britain, he ordered English and European dealers and traders to load his ships for the return trip with essential goods such as wine and, he ordered overseas traders to convert large amounts of ledger credits into specie—gold and silver coins—and ship it to America.

"Our exchange must inevitably come down very low," he explained to his factor in Cadiz, Spain, "and it will be of great advantage to have money coming in."[40]

Early in 1775, Britain's Parliament declared Massachusetts in rebellion and it ordered troops to land in Salem, Massachusetts, and seize rebel military supplies. In Richmond, Virginia, Patrick Henry responded by urging Americans to join the people of Massachusetts at war with Britain.

Speaking to his fellow assemblymen who had fled the provincial capital of Williamsburg to the sanctuary of St. John's Church in Richmond, he sounded words that would echo across America:

> "Our brethren are already in the field! Why stand we here idle?... Is life so dear, or peace so sweet, as to be purchased at the price of chains and slavery? Forbid it, Almighty God! I know not what course others may take, but as for me, give me liberty or give me death."[41]

Henry's words resounded beyond the American continent, across the Atlantic into the halls of Parliament, and across Europe. Parliament sent General Thomas Gage, the commanding general of British forces in Boston, orders to enforce the Coercive Acts to the letter.

Learning that nearby Concord was a major arms depot of the rebellious Provincial Assembly, Gage ordered a force of 700 troops to destroy or capture supplies in Concord, and, along their way, stop at Lexington to arrest rebel leaders John Hancock and Samuel Adams who had fled Boston to avoid capture.

On April 19, 1775, British troops reached Lexington, where they encountered 70 armed "Minutemen"[42] defending the green in the center of town. As the Minutemen began to retreat, a shot rang out—a shot that essayist Ralph Waldo Emerson would later memorialize poetically as "the shot heard round the world."[43] It set off a series of volleys that left eight Minutemen dead and ten others wounded—mostly farm boys and their fathers.

The shots at Lexington and the subsequent skirmish at Concord so incensed provincial leaders they immediately recalled the Continental Congress, which met three weeks later in Philadelphia to direct the war. It incorporated American troops near Boston as a Continental Army, asked other states to contribute troops to the army, and named George Washington, a Virginia militia colonel, as commanding general.

A week after Washington's appointment—and before he could assume command—British troops annihilated a 1,600-man American garrison on Bunker Hill, across the bay from Boston harbor.

Three weeks later, Congress reassembled In Philadelphia, where Quaker leader John Dickinson desperately sought to avert further conflict with Britain by preparing an "Olive Branch Petition" to the British king.

In it, the signatories pledged loyalty to the crown, but asserted constitutional rights as British subjects and pleaded with King George III to intervene to prevent Parliament from abridging those rights.

After the king scornfully rejected the petition Americans had little choice but to submit to military rule or prepare for war.

The Pennsylvania Assembly responded by forming a Committee of Safety to put the province on a war footing. Chaired occasionally by the aging Benjamin Franklin but more often by Robert Morris, the Committee voted to raise an army of 4,500 men, obtain ammunition for them (most men had their own arms), then form a provincial navy to guard the harbor and see to building forts along the Delaware River to protect Philadelphia against a sea-borne assault.

As committee demands increased, Robert Morris reached a point of near-exhaustion when an elfin 16-year-old—barely five feet tall—appeared seeking an apprenticeship.

Like Morris, John Swanwick had been born in Liverpool and sailed to America as an 11-year-old. He spoke German and French fluently and displayed an astonishing command of calculating skills and so reminded Morris of himself at that age that Morris hired him.

Within weeks, the hard-working boy had assumed enough of the firm's mundane tasks to free Morris to focus on provincial defense—and his family.

By the time Swanwick joined Willing Morris, Mary Morris had given birth to three more Morris babies. Their first born—Robert Morris III—was now five years old. The next oldest, Thomas Morris had been born in February, 1771; William White Morris, named for his uncle, had arrived in August 1772, and Hester had been born in July 1774.

As Swanwick proved himself able to handle most ordinary trading responsibilities—flour, tobacco, lumber shipments, etc.—Morris was able to focus on the purchase and shipment of arms and ammunition.

With imports of both forbidden by the British and subject to seizure, Morris had to devise an impossibly complex system of deception to purchase them overseas, ship them across the Atlantic, land them safely on American shores, and transport them to Pennsylvania troops.

His partner Thomas Willing, by then an influential member of Congress, convinced his colleagues that Morris and the Willing Morris firm was best positioned to do the job.

After considerable debate, Congress agreed and, in the largest munitions contract ever signed at the time, it advanced £80,000 in cash to Morris to buy 6,000 pounds of gunpowder and £30,000 for a second shipment, with Morris earning a profit of as much as 40 percent on each shipment.

Congress had no money of its own, of course, and not a single member dared even whisper the word "taxation" as a means of raising the necessary funds. Instead, Congress established a loan office to try borrowing funds at four percent, pledging only the full faith of Congress—a body that had no official standing.

Loans soon became impossible to obtain, however, leaving Congress with no choice but to print paper money—$6 million by the end of 1775, $4 million more in February 1776, $9 million more later in 1776. Congress pledged repayment with specie—gold or silver coins—on all issues.

Morris, of course, did lose a handful of ships at sea—usually for reasons unknown. They simply disappeared. The British captured a few; so did privateers and pirates, storms may have swallowed others, but the vast majority reached their destinations in Europe or the West Indies and returned safely with gunpowder, weapons ranging from muskets and rifles to cannons, lead for making shot, and supplies such as ships' hardware, sailcloth, and so forth.

Although most American suppliers suffered heavy losses to pirates and privateers, the ultra-modern Morris brigs were too swift and well-armed for renegade ships to present any serious threats. They were also quick to use a variety of subterfuges, hoisting flags of different nations—and even the skull and crossbones at times—to disguise their identities in whatever way they needed to discourage attack.

His largest ships—the two 200-ton brigs—were armed with one hundred guns; even his smallest sloops appeared well armed and vicious. His skills in fleet management would earn Willing Morris well over half the American foreign trade with France, Spain, and other European nations during the Revolutionary War.

Given his involvement in provincial government arms procurement, it was natural for Morris to seek a seat in the provincial assembly to help direct procurement efforts. By then both the provincial assembly and the Continental Congress met in the State House, and the affairs of both bodies—especially arms procurement—grew so entangled, that the Assembly named him to the Continental Congress in the fall of 1775.

Assuming most of the same duties in Congress that he commanded in the Assembly, Morris won election with Benjamin Franklin to a new Committee of Secret Correspondence. Ostensibly created for corresponding with friends of American autonomy in the British Parliament, it quickly devolved into a link with European enemies of Britain. It engaged secret agents abroad to establish such links—a simple task for Morris, with his many overseas ties—and the committee welcomed secret agents from those nations to the United States.

Just before Christmas 1775, a man calling himself a French business executive entered Philadelphia's State House with a letter of introduction to Robert Morris and other members of the Secret Committee. Feigning interest in establishing business ties with American merchants, Achard de Bonvouloir mentioned that French sentiment favored Americans in their dispute with Britain.

Although he said he could not speak for the French government, he expressed his strong belief that France was "well-disposed" toward the Americans and saw no obstacles to American merchants buying arms and other supplies from French merchants in exchange for American produce—tobacco, flour, rice, and the like.[44]

In effect, Bonvouloir gave Robert Morris an open invitation to begin a huge Franco-American trading operation that would serve his country's interests and more than offset any losses he might suffer in his trade with Britain during an America conflict with Britain.

Fearing that the beginning of Franco-American trade would provoke another world conflict, Franklin expressed reservations, saying he had traveled widely through the American provinces and failed to encounter any broad sentiment for separation from Britain.

By now a close associate of Franklin, Morris agreed, adding that among all those he knew, "Nobody wishes for independence.

> We love the people of England. We wanted no other friends, no other allies, but alas if they cannot be content to consider us as brothers entitled to the same freedom, the same privileges themselves enjoy, they cannot expect a people descended from their flesh and blood...to sit down tamely and see themselves stripped of all they hold dear.... I am now a member of the Continental Congress, and if I have any influence...it shall be exerted in favor of accommodation on terms consistent with our just claims, and if I thought there was anything asked on this side not founded in the Constitution, on reason and justice, I would oppose it. I will finish with sincerely praying that a speedy end may be put to the unhappy contest.[45]

With that, Robert Morris, against his better instincts, set to work preparing for war, establishing circuitous routes far off the customary shipping lanes to France to obtain arms and ammunition.

After eight of his ships reached France with full holds of much wanted tobacco and other produce, they returned with fifteen thousand French rifles and an assortment of big guns. Most were surplus materiel from the Seven Years' War, obsolete in Europe but perfectly usable by amateur American soldiers in the American wilderness.

By the end of 1775, Congress deferred to Morris's knowledge in maritime affairs to put him on the Marine Committee charged with building a navy.

Within weeks, he had converted four of his firm's cargo vessels into fighting ships and one of the Willing Morris piers in Philadelphia into a staging area. From there, he recruited four hundred men to man America's first fighting ships. He transferred one of his own 200-ton brigs to the Navy as its first warship and renamed it the *USS Alfred*.

Robert Morris's U.S.S. Alfred—America's first naval fighting ship.

His success on the Marine Committee and the energy he invested in his assignment earned him chairmanship of the Secret Committee charged with contracting arms and ammunition imports.

Some argued that the Morris appointment was akin to putting a fox in charge of a henhouse. Indeed, he was one of the signers of a committee order on February 19, 1776, advancing $200,000 to himself and four partners to purchase and transport American produce to Europe in exchange for arms and ammunition. He and his partners were to receive a five percent commission on the transaction.

Recognizing that his new four-vessel navy was no match for Britain's huge fleet, Morris sent his ships to attack minor, undefended

British ports in and about the Caribbean. His goal was to lure enough British ships from the main fleet to defend the outposts and leave the main fleet so weakened it would open more sea lanes for American cargo vessels to sail to and from Europe safely. His theory bore some dividends in early 1776, as Morris ships crossed the Atlantic and back safely carrying almost $200,000 worth of weapons, gunpowder, and cloth for making sails and tents.

A few delegates in congress grumbled as congressional funds poured into Willing Morris coffers, emerging at least in part as lavish displays of luxury and extravagant dinners at The Hills.

"The spirit of trade is avarice," growled Virginia's Richard Henry Lee, himself the owner of a sizable Virginia plantation whose mansion he had named *Chantilly,* after the elaborate 16th century Renaissance chateau north of Paris.

Morris scoffed at Lee's complaint, responding that his contract to handle the arms trade for Congress did not include an obligation to bankrupt himself and starve his family. He insisted he was entitled to a reasonable profit on the goods and services he supplied Congress—especially given the risks he took in ships sunk. In buying arms and ammunition, he pointed out, he was committing what the British government declared treason and was risking his life on the gallows.

"I did not, by becoming a delegate...relinquish my right of forming mercantile connections,"[46] Morris added. "I shall continue to discharge my duty faithfully to the public and pursue my private fortune by all such honorable and fair means as the times will admit of."

Then, in a sarcastic aside, he turned to Lee saying he had not noticed the Lee family cutting back on tobacco exports from their thousands of acres of Virginia plantations.[47]

The evident skills –indeed artistry—Morris displayed accomplishing any and every task the Congress had assigned him earned him seats on almost every important committee.

Besides the Secret Committee and Committee for Secret Correspondence, he sat on committees for naval affairs, trade regulations, ways and means, prisoner exchanges, treaty proposals, clothing acquisitions—indeed, so many that he emerged as one of the most powerful figures in Congress and one of the last voices of reason in the conflict with Britain.

"I am sorry to say," he wrote to Joseph Reed, a Philadelphia lawyer and member of Congress with Morris, "there are some amongst us that cannot bear the thought of reconciliation on any terms. To these men, all propositions of the kind sound like high treason....

> "I cannot help condemning this disposition as it must be founded in keen resentment or on interested views whereas we ought to have the interest of our country and the good of mankind to act as the main spring in all our conduct.... It is our duty...to weigh well the consequences of every determination we come to and in short to lay aside all prejudices, resentments, and sanguine notions of our own strength in order that reason may influence and wisdom guide our councils.... Why should we fear to treat of peace?"[48]

On June 7, 1776, Virginia's Richard Henry Lee stood before Congress with a small piece of paper he held in his hand, from which he read aloud:

Resolved:

> That these United Colonies are, and of right ought to be, free and independent States, that they are absolved from all allegiance to the British crown, and that all political connection between them and the State of Great Britain is, and ought to be totally dissolved.[49]

After he had finished reading it, a majority voted enthusiastically in favor of it—almost all except Robert Morris, who shocked the Congress by joining with partner Thomas Willing and Quaker leader John Dickinson by voting "Nay." Nearly a month later, Robert Morris, Jr., who had asserted that commerce ought to be "free as the air" sat resolute in his startling opposition to the declaration.

Declaring it "an improper time" for independence, he warned that too many Americans remained loyal to Britain; the issue of separation "has caused division when we wanted union." With that, America's richest man—and one of its most powerful—seemed intent on ending the quest for independence.

Chapter 4

'DEATH AND RUIN STARE US IN THE FACE'

O

n July 2, 1776, Congress ignored the objections of Robert Morris and resumed its quest for independence by voting on a new and more elaborate Declaration of Independence. Morris and Dickinson abruptly stood and left the hall.

When Congress finished voting, twelve states had voted in favor of independence, with one state abstaining. New York delegates said they needed to await instructions on how to vote from their state assemblies.

Bold newspaper headlines confirmed the vote, and John Adams of Massachusetts, who had seconded Richard Henry Lee's resolution, wrote to his wife Abigail predicting that July 2, 1776 would become "the most memorable epocha [sic] in the history of America.... This will cement the Union and avoid those heats and perhaps convulsions which might have been occasioned by such a declaration six months ago."[50]

Robert Morris disagreed. Citing deep divisions among Americans regarding their individual ties to Britain. "I have uniformly voted against and opposed the declaration of independence," he explained, "because in my poor opinion it was an improper time."

Although the press had declared America independent on July 2, the document declaring independence bore but two signatures—that of John Hancock, the president of the Continental Congress, and John Thompson, the secretary of Congress who witnessed the Hancock signature."

Although copies were sent to all the state assemblies, it would take weeks, perhaps months, before they could or would ratify the document and make it official. Until then, America remained British, and all reports from the battlefield indicated it would remain that way in the foreseeable future.

Even as delegates were debating whether to ratify the Declaration, 130 British ships sailed into New York Bay and landed more than 30,000 British and Hessian troops on Staten Island. On August 27, 20,000 of them stormed ashore across the bay in Brooklyn and all but annihilated Patriot troops.

On September 15, five British ships pounded American emplacements on Manhattan island, sending 6,000 of the 8,000 terror-stricken Connecticut militiamen on guard sprinting to the rear without firing a shot.

"Good God," Washington cried out. "Are these the men with which I am to defend America?"[51]

Congress grew so distraught over the military setbacks that they accepted what they believed to be an offer of a cease-fire by the British high command.

When Benjamin Franklin, John Adams, and Edmund Rutledge of South Carolina arrived at British headquarters to talk peace, however, the British commanders told them revocation of the Declaration of Independence was a precondition to any talks. The three emissaries returned to Philadelphia humiliated, all but vindicating the earlier Morris argument that it was "an improper time" to declare independence.

In July, however, Pennsylvanians replaced their anti-independence delegation in the Continental Congress with delegates willing to sign the Declaration of Independence. They made one exception, however, by re-electing Robert Morris—and with good reason.

Even with his negative vote the pro-independence delegates would have a firm majority. Moreover, Congress would have no means—or hope—of raising money to pay Washington's troops or establish credit to buy war materiel to fight the British without Morris money and his international trading apparatus.

Taken aback by his re-election, Morris returned to Congress reluctantly, explaining that "although my interest and inclination prompt me to decline the service, I cannot depart from one point which first induced me to enter the public line...that it is the duty of every individual to act his part in whatever station his country may call him in times of danger and distress."[52]

Thus, on August 2, 1776, Morris declared war against his native land, joining most of the 56 other signers in adding his name to America's Declaration of Independence. Having done so, he put aside all qualms he may have had about the conflict and went to war against Britain with a ferocity, tenacity, and courage that few champions of American independence, save George Washington himself, would match.

With the famous financier's signature on the document, Congress was able to raise $20 million in cash and float $40 million worth of paper in Europe to pay for arming and clothing the Continental Army.

"The creditors trust the union," Morris commented. "The financial strength of the states "is derived from their union."[53]

As Morris touted the benefits of union, a curious "Frenchman" appeared at the doors of Congress to voice full agreement with and all but embrace Morris and his poinr of view. Announcing himself as Achard de Bonvouloir, a merchant from Antwerp, Belgium, he met with as many signers as he could, saying he supported their collective quest for independence, and believed the French court was also "well-disposed" towards them.

Asserting he had no official ties to the French government, he nonetheless said he saw "no obstacles" to private transactions for American merchants to buy arms and other military supplies from French merchants in exchange for produce—tobacco, rice, and the like.

In fact, Bonvouloir was the French army's most accomplished secret intelligence officer, dispatched to America by Foreign Minister Charles Gravier, Comte de Vergennes.

Intent on avenging his nation's defeat by the British in the Seven Years' War, Vergennes charged Bonvouloir with assessing the depth of the intent and strength of American secessionist forces and the type of military aid that might help ensure their victory.

France had been left on the verge of bankruptcy by the Seven Years' War and could ill afford engaging in another war with Britain. By providing surreptitious aid in the form of military equipment and prolonging the American Revolution, Vergennes hoped to tie down the British military, sap its strength, and open the way for a French force to invade and reclaim Canada.

After meeting with Robert Morris and other signers, Bonvouloir returned to France and assured Vergennes that American secessionists were prepared to fight to the last man to gain independence. Eager to rid French army depots of outdated (albeit functional) war materiel and given that the costs of doing so were negligible, Vergennes met with Connecticut merchant-banker[54] Silas Deane—the envoy of Congress who doubled as Morris's Paris agent.

In the end, the French minister agreed to ship surplus arms, ammunition, and clothing for 25,000 men and one hundred field pieces to the Americans.

Like Morris and other merchant-bankers in Congress, Deane's motive for supporting independence had less to do with independence than it did with forcing Britain to end taxation in America. Like Morris, too, the war presented him with an irresistible money-making opportunity that he could cloak with a veneer of patriotism. Indeed, Robert Morris had encouraged him:

"It seems to me that the present oppert'y [opportunity] of improving our fortunes ought not to be lost," Morris opine, "especially as the very means of doing it will contribute to the service of our country at the same time."

In addition to costs of French supplies, Congress had pledged to pay Deane's expenses and a commission of five percent. After Deane closed the deal with Vergennes, Morris all but drooled as he wrote, "If we have but luck in getting the goods safely to America, the profits will be sufficient [for] us all."[55]

Perhaps. What was more certain was the trust creditors placed in Morris. The Morris vaults—at his pier-side headquarters, at his overseas facilities, at his multiple homes, and at Morris-only-knew-where-else—had accumulated untold millions of dollars in specie—that is, cash and precious metals. In addition, merchants across America, Britain, and Europe held "ledger credits" worth hundreds of millions of dollars for goods they had received from Morris and resold, and from which he could draw to buy more goods or simply convert to cash.

With his signature on the Declaration of Independence, Morris immediately used his enormous international trading network, his huge armed fleet (the world's largest), and his bulging treasury to fill Continental Army needs. His trading network spanned Europe, reaching almost every port, through which his ships, flying a myriad of different flags, passed all but unnoticed by the watchful eyes of sailors in the crow's nests of British ships.

Scores of ports in the Caribbean served as transfer points, where Morris agents could break up large military shipments from Europe and reload them onto sleek, small and swift sloops that raced along the Atlantic coast, in, out, and around the Outer Banks and into tiny inlets, impenetrable by the bigger, slower, hostile British boats.

Because of the complexity of his new trade, Morris added new chief agents at key points of his network—all of them intelligent, well-to-do, well-educated men with backgrounds in trading and motivated in part by material gain but as much by patriotism and a love of adventure.

Philadelphia's William Bingham was typical. The son of a wealthy trader, he boasted two degrees from the College of Philadelphia (later, University of Pennsylvania) and owned a successful trading company and his own fleet of cargo vessels which plied the French Caribbean.

While secretly taking command of some Morris operations, he also established ties as a diplomatic liaison to French authorities.

A presence at all major social functions for foreign diplomats in the region, Bingham was able to purchase military goods secretly from a dozen or more European nations—and from privateers—offering them shiploads of highly prized American tobacco in exchange. Within weeks, Bingham had shipped ten thousand muskets and the requisite gunpowder north to Washington's army. He also sent shiploads of linens, clothing, and other items labeled civilian household goods to Morris American depots, where Morris agents distributed them to various Continental Army encampments.

Morris established other aides in Spain, Hamburg, New Orleans, and Boston. He sent his half-brother Thomas to France to work with Connecticut merchant Silas Deane.

"He has been a wild youth heretofore," Morris admitted about his brother, "but if he is now sensible of former follies, he may be the more valuable man for it." Morris said Thomas had convinced him that he had "discarded all his follies."[56]

With Morris agents bidding for war material across the Atlantic world, prices for military supplies and American tobacco, rice, and ships' masts soared. Although British warships captured or sank some Morris cargo ships, his fleet destroyed far more ships than it lost. One Morris sloop with eighteen six-pound guns overwhelmed three British ships en route from Europe to the Caribbean, adding a trio of handsome vessels to the Morris fleet.

The huge trading network that Morris created produced enormous profits. Operating like a hyperactive octopus, its tentacles reached into every European country and Caribbean island. To feed Europe's appetite for tobacco, Morris cornered the American market and used the tobacco he bought to buy stocks of European military supplies.

"I have much in my power or under my influence both public and private," Morris boasted. "My desire is to serve justly and fairly every interest I am connected with." Although Morris had fervently embraced patriotism, he embraced capitalism with equal fervor.

As Morris's monetary fortune grew, however, Washington's military fortune shrank dramatically. After humiliating Washington's troops in Brooklyn, British troops had chased the Americans out of New York and westward across New Jersey's wilderness into sheets of icy autumn rains that threatened to freeze the retreat. Then, as they stared at imminent defeat, the men of two brigades stunned the general by declaring their enlistment periods at an end and fleeing camp for home. Suddenly, the Continental Army shrank to a mere 4,000 men, of whom only 1,000 remained fit to fight. The crushing military setback forced fleeing survivors to leave their food supplies, tents and blankets, and most of their ammunition behind.

"Our people knew not the hardships and calamities of war when they so boldly dared Britain to arms," Morris fumed when he heard of the troop desertions. "Every man then was a bold patriot....but now when...death and ruin stare us in the face...many of those who were foremost in noise, shrink coward-like from the danger."[57]

On December 12, 1776, enemy troops galloped within sight of Philadelphia, and Congress fled to Baltimore, all but conceding defeat. Morris, along with George Clymer, a Philadelphia merchant, and Georgia lawyer George Walton, a fierce proponent of independence, refused to flee, deciding instead to remain and form a shadow government to negotiate with the British if and when they occupied the city.

In fact, Morris could not have left without burning down his homes and his huge enterprise to prevent the British from seizing the properties and their contents. Apart from untold millions in coins, cash, bank notes, promissory notes and valuables in the Morris vaults, stacks of irreplaceable private and public documents revealed the identities, finances, and transactions of traders across the globe, including, prominent Americans in and out of Congress. In addition,

Morris had been conducting much of the government's financial affairs from his counting house, where he kept all official papers.

So when Congress fled to Baltimore, John Hancock, the President of Congress, "empowered" Morris and the aging Benjamin Franklin "to direct all matters on behalf of the United States of America, the other members of said committee being now absent."[58]

But the infirmities of old age kept the 70-year-old Franklin confined, leaving Morris to govern the nation alone. In addition to the government's commerce and financial affairs, Morris assumed authority over the navy and all merchant ships sailing in and out of Philadelphia harbor—many of them his own, of course. With his incoming ships conveying almost all war materiel, Morris was, in effect, America's unofficial minister of war,

"I have much in my power...both public and private," Morris admitted. "My desire is to serve justly and faithfully every interest I am connected with."[59]

Although Morris drew his share of critics for exceeding the scope of his authority, John Hancock, the President of Congress, had nothing but high praise for him.

"Congress seems unanimously sensible of the obligations which they owe you," he wrote to Morris, "and you may boast of being the only man whom they all... think well of."[60] Indeed, when Hancock's health began to fade a few months later, delegates asked Morris to replace him as president of Congress, but he declined.

When Morris learned of the Continental Army's humiliating retreat across New Jersey, he ordered seizure of hundreds of blankets and a variety of war materiel to send to Washington's army. He sent $100,000 of his own funds to Washington to buy more supplies and pledged, "If further occasional supplies are necessary, you may depend on my exertions either in a public or private capacity."[61]

But the aid arrived too late to halt Washington's retreat.

"It is impossible," Washington wrote to his brother, "to give you any idea...of my difficulties–and the constant perplexities and mortification I constantly meet with."[62] And in a letter to his cousin who, in the general's absence, had agreed to supervise Washington's 40,000-acre Virginia plantation, Washington complained, "Your imagination can scarce extend to a situation more distressing than mine.... I think the game is pretty well up, from disaffection and want of spirit and fortitude. The inhabitants instead of resistance are offering submission."[63]

The game seemed pretty well up elsewhere as well. An expedition into Canada that Washington had authorized had met with disaster earlier in 1776 with the death of the American commanding general, 100 American troops dead or wounded, and more than 300 taken prisoner.

Washington had no sooner dispatched his letter to Mount Vernon when British troops chased his exhausted little army to the east bank of the Delaware River. With a choice of surrendering or crossing the ice laden waters to the Pennsylvania shore, Washington chose the latter, ordering his men to retrieve every boat they could find along the eastern shore to prevent further pursuit by the British.

Although they arrived safely on the west bank of the river, they were exhausted. Many had left their weapons behind; most had run out of ammunition, and almost all had lost the will to fight after receiving no pay during their days on the run. In desperation, Washington again turned to Robert Morris.

They were a curious pair—the fat, jolly, garrulous extrovert and the tall, austere, steely mouthed soldier, always, it seemed, standing silently—at attention. Morris and Washington had first met in the spring of 1773, when Washington was traveling through Philadelphia to New York. They met again at the Continental Congress, and Morris invited Washington to dine at The Hills, where they formed a warm friendship, with Mary Morris establishing strong ties to Martha Washington.

When, in December 1776, Morris learned of Washington's plight on the banks of the Delaware, he responded immediately. Racing to the Philadelphia docks, he commandeered every wagon in sight and ordered his men to enter nearby homes and seize every blanket, article of clothing, and weapon they could find, along with ammunition, for transport up the Delaware River to Washington's camp.

Two weeks later, as the bitter cold of Christmas night penetrated the early hours of December 26, 1776, 2,400 of Washington's healthiest men, clothed and rearmed by Robert Morris, rose as one and, with the general in the lead boat, pushed off into the ice-choked waters through the storm and crossed the Delaware River, landing on a sandy bank just north of Trenton.

Fired by outrage over the British king's hiring of Hessian mercenaries to fight Britain's war, the Americans surged into Trenton while the Hessians were still abed sleeping off Christmas night revelry As the Americans stormed up King Street, firing at anything that moved, a Hessian stepped outside his barracks and saw the Americans approaching.

"Der Feind! Der Feind!" he cried out. "The enemy! The enemy!"

"Heraus! Heraus!"—"Turn out! Turn out!"

The terrified Hessians raced out into the snowstorm in night clothes and staggered through deep snow toward their artillery emplacements at the top of King Street.

Washington, however, had anticipated their moves and sent a 50-man squad to circle to the rear of town and capture the Hessian cannons that stared down the street at the advancing Americans. The two officers who led the daring raid fell wounded defending the cannons—one of them a distant Washington cousin, Captain William Washington; the other, Lieutenant James Monroe, the future

American President. Monroe had temporarily abandoned his university studies in Virginia to enlist in the Virginia militia.

General Washington decorated and promoted both young men for their heroism in ensuring what became one of the signal military victories in American history: the surrender of the entire 1,000-man Hessian force and cession of Trenton to the Americans.

With Washington's improbable victory at Trenton, American spirits soared—civilians and soldiers alike. News of the victories spread across the American landscape, across the Atlantic to Britain and over the English Channel to Europe. Morris exulted—until he received word from Washington that the troops who had attacked Trenton had left nearly 2,000 of their comrades behind. All were suffering in the frigid weather without adequate blankets or clothing, without arms to fight the enemy, and—still worse—without food. All had been unpaid for months and sought only the strength to desert.

"If it be possible, sir, to give us assistance, do it," Washington wrote to Morris. "Borrow money while it can be done. We are doing it upon our private credit. Every man of interest and every lover of his country must strain his credit upon such an occasion. No time, my dear sir, is to be lost."[64]

The "we" in Washington's note, of course, was Washington himself, who had spent his own cash reserves to pay the troops who attacked Trenton.

With the initial moneys from Congress spent organizing the army, Congress was without funds, and Washington had had to use his own money to pay some of the troops. Although not as wealthy as Morris, he was owner of one of America's largest and most successful tobacco plantations, with more than 300 slaves and substantial cash reserves and trader credits.

Coming after Washington's stunning victory at Trenton, Washington's message stunned Morris, who rushed this note to the general:

> I am up very early this morning to dispatch a supply of fifty thousand dollars to your excellency.... The year 1776 is over. I am heartily glad of it & hope you nor America will never be plagued with such another. Let us accept the success at Trenton as a presage of future fortunate events.[65]

Amazed and elated by Morris's quick and remarkable responss—Washington called it "Magick Money"—he led his men from Trenton to Princeton to try to catch the British encampment off guard.

In one of the most clever maneuvers of his military career, Washington ordered troops to set up a mock encampment, complete with tents and burning campfires well outside Princeton. They then stole away quietly into the darkness of a nearby forest.

As British troops surrounded what they believed was Washington's encampment ablaze with campfires, Washington's men surrounded them and forced them to surrender their arms. He ordered the humiliated British commander to retreat eastward to Brunswick, leaving Princeton and much of western New Jersey in Patriot hands.

Washington's improbable victories at Trenton and Princeton sent American spirits soaring—civilians and soldiers alike. News of the victories spread across the American landscape, across the Atlantic to Britain and Europe. Morris sent his congratulations:

"Heaven," he wrote to Washington, "has blessed you with a firmness of mind, Steadiness of countenance and patience in sufferings that give you infinite advantages of other men."[66]

The Morris letter was "so highly pleasing" to Washington that he replied with uncharacteristic emotion:

"Be assured, Sir, that nothing would add more to my satisfaction than an unreserved Correspondence with a Gentleman of whose abilities and attachment to the Cause we are contending for, I entertain so high opinion of as I do yours"[67]

Unexpected news from Europe, however, changed Morris's mood dramatically. His brother Thomas, whom Robert had entrusted with overseeing congressional business in Europe, had quit his Paris office, absconding with £1,000, embezzling £36,000 in Willing Morris funds, and re-emerging in a drunken stupor in London.

Scottish merchant John Ross, a Robert Morris trading partner, reported finding Thomas Morris "drunk at least 22 hours out of every 24 and never without one or two whores in company....abandoned to the most disgraceful pursuits of debauchery...with Reptiles of human society."[68]

Thomas Willing, Morris's partner of twenty years, warned his old friend, "We shall be disgraced,"[69] to which Morris responded by covering his brother's debts and embezzlements and apologizing to his partner, his overseas agents, and members of Congress.

With the British pushed out of Princeton and back to the Jersey shore, Congress returned to Philadelphia—only to find that the British had launched a new, more formidable multi-front effort to crush the American insurgency.

In the North, the British launched a three-pronged effort to isolate New England from the other colonies. As 8,000 troops moved southward from Canada, a second force was moving eastward from western New York, while a third force had started northward on the Hudson River from New York City to link with the other two forces at Albany, New York.

Meanwhile, the British envisioned sending a fleet to sail into and up Chesapeake Bay, where they would land south of Philadelphia, march to that city and capture the leaders of the Revolution, along with the American fleet, and America's largest center of banking and trade. The capture of Philadelphia, the British believed, would extinguish the last sparks of resistance to British rule.

At first, the British military strategy proved brilliant—indeed, flawless. Fifteen thousand British troops sailed south from New York Bay in mid-July, entering and sailing up Chesapeake Bay and landing 50 miles south of Philadelphia. Although American civilian leaders had fled and escaped capture, the British took full control of Philadelphia by the end of September, then humiliated Washington and his army at nearby Germantown, and forced the remnants of the American army to flee to a barren mountaintop plateau at Valley Forge, Pennsylvania. There, Washington and his Americans faced near starvation during one of the coldest winters in memory.

Again, American troops began deserting, and again, Washington pleaded with leaders of Congress and with state governors for money to pay his men. When those pleas went unheeded. he once more turned to Robert Morris, who all but emptied his Philadelphia cash reserves to pay and find food for Washington's men.

Meanwhile, most members of Congress had fled to their homes after British troops marched into Philadelphia. Virginia's Richard Henry Lee, however, had led an intrepid band of twenty delegates—enough for a quorum—westward to Lancaster, Pennsylvania, where he re-established the bare bones of a Congress and the Confederation government.

A day after arriving, though, Lee determined the town to be too unprotected against British assault, and he led the Congress further westward across the raging Susquehanna River rapids to the frontier town of York, where he believed the dangerous river crossing would discourage British pursuit.

Intent on remaining with Congress but unwilling to settle his pregnant wife and four children in York's primitive lodgings, Morris purchased an oversized mansion called "The Castle," north of York in Mannheim.

Built by the brilliant albeit eccentric German glass manufacturer Baron Heinrich Wilhelm Stiegel, it went for sale when Stiegel went bankrupt. Morris now snapped it up, along with its rare tapestries and elegant furnishings. A caravan of covered wagons carried Morris and his family, household staff and slaves, and their personal and household possessions to his new home from the Elms, where they had taken refuge after the British occupied Philadelphia.

The Castle's luxurious European-style comforts immediately transformed the Morris family's exile from Philadelphia into a pleasant holiday. It allowed Mary a serene pregnancy, gave the children endless fields and woods to explore, and transformed Morris into the most influential member of Congress. An invitation to escape York's discomforts on a weekend stay at the Morris Castle was a coveted prize that allowed Morris to "recruit," in a sense, almost every delegate to his way of thinking and give him all-but-total control of the provisional American government.

At Morris's urging, Congress recognized the folly of directing a war by committees. It replaced the most important one with what was the nation's first executive post—Superintendent of Finance—and it immediately named Morris to the post. Equivalent to today's Secretary of the Treasury, it vested Morris with sweeping executive powers.

In effect, Robert Morris assumed virtually dictatorial control of the entire government such as it was. He immediately cut spending and forced members of Congress to discharge sinecures.

He gathered all government accounting under his aegis and introduced competitive bidding on government contracts. He threatened to use the power of his firm in the marketplace to drive hoarders out of business and forced dealers to release supplies to Washington's troops at Valley Forge. He sent veiled threats to state governors—many of them merchants or planters—to fund the war or risk unstated penalties in the markets for their services or goods. Some actually responded with contributions of funds or commodities.

The extent of his power became all but absolute when, without a word to Washington or Congress, he ordered an armed force down the Mississippi to New Orleans to obtain gunpowder for the Continental Army and destroy as many enemy posts as possible along way.

To raise more cash to pay Washington's troops, Morris printed it. As America's richest man, his name and signature on paper money made it almost as good as gold.

"Paper," of course, was as old as the colonies themselves. Most 17 and 18th century settlers had arrived penniless. Although they could often claim land in the wilderness without funds, clearing land and planting crops required making payments to merchants for supplies and seeds. They did so with I.O.U.'s, which merchants, in turn, cashed out, when those same settlers brought their crops to market in the ensuing years. Merchants in America resold the crops to British merchants who issued "ledger credits," with which the Americans could buy agricultural supplies, household furnishings and other items produced in Britain to resell in the American market.

As British subjects in British colonies, therefore, Americans needed almost no specie, or hard money, for the first two centuries of their existence. All handwritten IOU's were the equivalent of today's checks, backed by each check-writer's goods or services. George Washington routinely ordered fine china and furniture for his Mount Vernon home and costly linens for himself and Martha in exchange for tobacco shipments. And when Congress first needed funds, it printed what it needed, with troops and merchants accepting the so-called "continental dollars" knowing they had been issued by the nation's wealthiest men.

Benjamin Franklin had no difficulty paying merchants with his handwritten I.O. U.'s, but Morris, when faced with paying thousands of troops, decided to issue carefully designed, printed bills resembling currencies of established nations. They were worth no more than ordinary I.O.U.s, but they looked like money, the troops accepted them as payment, and they grew so common place that they earned nicknames as "Big Bobs," for $1,000 notes, and "Little Bobs" for $10 notes.

Despite his other-worldly skills manipulating funds, Morris eventually had to tap his personal treasure to fill the Washington army's voracious appetite for arms and ammunition and the need for ever more troops. In the end, Morris spent £10 million of his own money to pay Washington's men. To pay for overseas purchases, he tapped his reserves of ledger credits at Europe's leading merchants worth at least as much.

By summer's end, Washington seemed likely to lose his command, as British forces swept across the Northeast, sprinting southward along Lake Champlain to Albany to meet a second British force marching eastward along the Mohawk River. A third force from New York was sailing northward on the Hudson River to close ranks with the other two forces just as the American Northern Army ran out of ammunition. Surrender would allow the British to sever New England and New York from the rest of the American colonies.

With British forces occupying Philadelphia and Washington's pathetic little army paralyzed by hunger and cold at Valley Forge, the British army would have free rein to sweep across New Jersey, Delaware, Maryland and Virginia and end America's war of independence.

Chapter 5

'A GLORIOUS AND HAPPY DAY'

J ust as the British military command was about to celebrate the end of war in America, an unmarked 300-ton ship appeared at the entrance of Portsmouth harbor in New Hampshire and raised the French flag.

Stunned at first, townsfolk raised a cheer and raced to the pier—men, women, and children—all embraced the crew of French sailors and helped them offload 12,000 muskets, 50 brass cannon, powder and ammunition, 1,000 tents, and clothes for 10,000 troops. They then loaded the supplies onto a wagon train that immediately began rolling westward towards Bennington, Vermont.

As the first wagons reached Bennington, American militiamen refilled their powder horns and, with new weapons in their hands, stopped the advance of a 1,000-man British force, killing 200 and capturing 700.

By mid-October, the re-armed and reinvigorated Americans under General Horatio Gates had marched the forty miles to Saratoga, New York, where they out-gunned and out-maneuvered the powerful British army and forced the surrender of 5,700 smartly dressed British troops and their fabled General John—"Gentleman Johnny"—Burgoyne.

The French ship that reached Portsmouth was the first of three that Morris agent Silas Deane had arranged with a

shadowy French firm that the French king had ordered to carry surplus French Army military supplies to American forces. The other two never arrived in America.

Although most Americans cheered the Gates victory, a handful of disgruntled officials cited Gates's success as grounds for appointing him to succeed Washington in the wake of the latter's continuing battlefield failures. Morris all but galloped from his castle to York to crush what seemed a cabal to unseat Washington.

"I really think it is a horrid thing that mankind should ever support such unworthy attacks on worthy characters," Morris exclaimed. "The General will not suffer alone in any loss of character; his country and his country's cause will inevitably suffer.... Let us therefore withstand these attempts against the first man in this world and unite our endeavors to procure him such force as will enable him to shine with the splendor he merits."[70]

Morris had no sooner crushed dissent against Washington than word arrived of more misbehavior and malfeasance by his brother Thomas Morris in Europe. The disclosures left Morris little choice but to act swiftly and decisively. After covering his brother's losses, he sent Thomas this letter: "We have received authentic information that you have unhappily preferred dissipation to business and are so bent on the pursuit of pleasures as to be an improper Agent.... You are therefore hereby dismissed."[71]

A few weeks later, on January 31, 1778, 28-year-old Thomas Morris was found dead.

To salvage his standing in Congress, Morris sent an apology to the President of Congress Henry Laurens: "Could I have had the least idea of what has happened, I would sooner have perished than he should be trusted.

> My distress is more than I can describe. To think that in the midst of the most ardent entreaties I was capable of making to promote the interest & welfare of my country I should be

the means of introducing a worthless wretch to disgrace and discredit it, is too much to bear.[72]

Before the year ended, Laurens accepted the Morris apology, and most delegates in Congress put aside concerns about the Thomas Morris scandal when word arrived that the king of France was preparing to recognize American independence if the provinces united and formed an actual nation.

On November 15, 1777, Congress sought to do just that by approving Articles of Confederation that created the "United States of America."

Although ratification by all state governments would not come until March, 1781, Morris threw aside any lingering hopes for reconciliation with Britain and signed the Articles in March 1778, after French king Louis XVI recognized the new nation and ensured American victory.

Aware of imminent French engagement in the war, the British withdraw from Philadelphia to consolidate northern forces in New York. As the British began their march northward, Washington sent a contingent of troops under Brigadier General Benedict Arnold to seize control of Philadelphia and prevent looting. Meanwhile, Washington led the rest his men out of Valley Forge to follow and harass the British column as it moved northward through New Jersey towards New York.

Eager to survey the damage wrought by British occupation in Philadelphia, Robert Morris joined Benedict Arnold. As they approached the city, the damage proved far worse than they had anticipated. The British had burned homes on country estates outside the city, including the beautiful Morris mansion at "The Hills." Only a shell of his home remained. Troops had cut down the trees that surrounded it and ripped up fences for firewood.

Nor was the city spared. One resident described the city as "greatly desolated...death and sore destruction has overtaken and impends over so many."[73] Finding his own home uninhabitable, Morris hired a crew of workers to begin repairs, then returned to Mannheim to rejoin his family.

Towards the end of June 1778, harassment by Washington's troops forced the British army to halt its northward march 20 miles northeast of Philadelphia at Monmouth Courthouse and engage the Americans. A day of exhausting heroics by both sides produced indecisive results, and, as darkness set in, Washington's troops bedded down for the night. While they slept, the British quietly slipped away to Sandy Hook, a spit of land on the northern New Jersey shore at the entrance to New York Bay, where they ceded New Jersey to the Americans and boarded transport ships to New York.

Washington claimed a victory at Monmouth Courthouse, calling it "a glorious and happy day" that cost the British "at least 2000 of their best troops. We had 60 men killed."[74]

By July 4, Robert Morris and his family were able to return to Philadelphia to celebrate the anniversary of American independence. Congress resumed its deliberations on July 7, and five days later, the city erupted in joyful celebrations to welcome the French fleet and the French ambassador—the first such foreign emissary—to the world's newest nation, the United States of America.

On board with the French ambassador was Silas Deane, the Connecticut merchant and former member of Congress, who had negotiated the financial terms of the multi-million-dollar French aid to the American army.

Although Congress had allowed Deane to extract a commission of five percent, accusations arose that he had pocketed far more and engaged in "private schemes"—some with Robert Morris's disgraced brother Thomas Morris—to "plunder...the public money.[75]

Congress, therefore, asked Deane to return to America with all pertinent documents and receipts associated with the French aid.

The rumors of Deane's alleged malfeasance inevitably spawned questions about Robert Morris, who had partnered with Deane in many business transactions before Deane had left for Europe. When, therefore, Deane arrived without a scrap of paper to document his disposition of funds, Congress was outraged.

"Would anybody have supposed that a gentleman in the character of a commercial agent and afterwards in that of a public minister would return home after seeing himself recalled...and not bring with him his papers and vouchers?" asked polemicist Thomas Paine, then in the employ of Congress as a foreign affairs liaison.

"Neither has he yet accounted for his expenditure of public money, which...might have been done by a written statement of accounts.... There is something in this concealment of papers," Paine charged, "that looks like embezzlement!"[76]

What Paine saw as malfeasance, however, Robert Morris and the powerful merchant-bankers who dominated Congress saw as legitimate profit opportunities in financial transactions they brokered between governments. Although Paine argued that such profiteering was criminal behavior, few members of Congress had not profited from contracts to supply arms, ammunition, clothing, linens, tobacco, flour, and food to the army. Indeed, every merchant, banker, and planter—in and out of Congress—who could profit from the war did so quite openly—including Robert Morris.

Even George Washington, who made a show of refusing any salary as commander-in-chief of the Continental Army, continued selling and profiting from sales of tobacco and other crops from his 40,000-acre Mount Vernon, Virginia, plantation. Plantation disbursements at Mount Vernon reached more than £66,000 in 1780, while assets included a cash balance of £17,000 before receipts from 1780 crops.

In addition, Washington remained one of America's most prominent land speculators, claiming thousands of acres of raw land in the wilderness west of the Appalachians in Pennsylvania and Ohio. Far from being considered unethical, speculation in land for resale to prospective farmers was a primary—and honored—occupation for almost all of America's Founding Fathers and many other leading merchants, bankers, and landowners. Lands in the wilderness were there for the taking—and those who could take, took.

Few prominent Americans with funds at their disposal did not find ways to profit from the Revolution. Even the sacrosanct Ben Franklin returned from France having drained £100,000 from his congressional account. When questioned by a member of Congress about the absent funds, Franklin fired back with scripture: "Muzzle not the ox that treadeth out his master's grain."[77] No one in Congress—nor, for that matter, Washington—ever mentioned the shortage again.

As for Morris, he had owned interests in many of the privateers that haunted the seas, seizing cargoes and crews without regard for national origin, then reselling the cargoes, ransoming captives, and refitting captured ships for his own fleet. His fleet now numbered more than 250 ships—the world's largest.

Although he acquired and refitted almost as many more as warships for the fledgling American navy, he kept his own fleet busy smuggling cargoes to and from American ports or roaming the seas as privateers, seizing British cargo ships. Because he had funded ninety-five percent of the government's wartime expenses, his profits from privateering and private commercial ventures left him "about even" financially he said when he left Congress at the end of 1778.

Nonetheless, Paine expressed dismay after learning how widespread profiteering by Founding Fathers had become. Governed by a set of his own unique moral principles, Paine had contributed all his rather meager earnings as a pamphleteer to Congress for the war effort.

Penniless as the war drew to a close, he rebuked delegates in Congress and almost every military leader for not doing the same.

"To what degree of corruption must we sink," Paine demanded to know, "if our delegates and ambassadors are to be admitted on a private partnership in trade? Such a connection unfits a delegate for his duty in Congress by making him a partner with the servant over whose conduct he sits as one of his judges....... No wonder that Mr. Deane should be so violently supported by the members [of Congress].[78]

Morris replied angrily. The ultimate champion of free enterprise unfettered by government competition, regulations, taxes, or interference of any kind, Morris reasserted his right to profit from his office and denied the right of Congress "to inquire into what mercantile connection I have had or now have with Mr. Deane, or with any other person."[79]

By then, however, the continuous carping and criticisms had exacted a high toll on Morris and his family life—as had the costs of war on his finances. In January 1779, after Morris had received potentially lucrative opportunities to return to private business, he asked Congress to replace him. Congress protested that he was leaving the new American nation without funds to continue the war. It sought to placate him by abruptly ending all inquiries into his finances and even firing Thomas Paine. But Morris was adamant and left Congress to focus on his family and his business.

With the return of high—and low—society to Philadelphia, the work of rebuilding the city and restoring day-to-day life produced a wave of public and private spending, spurring sharp price increases and a drop in the value of the Continental (i.e., American) dollar.

Without Morris to enforce fiscal and monetary discipline, Congress deteriorated into a snake pit of arguments—as often as not on how to settle the fate of Silas Deane. Rather than get trapped in political recriminations, South Carolina's Henry Laurens resigned as President of Congress.

Washington, if few others, made a show of disapproval at the political turmoil. "Speculation, peculation, and an insatiable thirst for riches seem to have got the better of every other consideration and almost every order of men," the general railed. "Party disputes and personal quarrels are the great business of the day whilst the momentous concerns of an empire...are but secondary considerations and postponed.... I am alarmed and wish to see my countrymen roused."[80]

Although determined to abandon national politics and focus on rebuilding his business, Morris soon found himself sucked into Pennsylvania state politics, agreeing to become a member of the state assembly to help put down the class war that was erupting in Philadelphia.

The war with Britain had forced Congress to add to the already deep pile of unsecured paper by printing tens of millions of paper dollars to buy war supplies. As the value of paper dropped, consumers needed more and more of the paper to buy things. Prices quoted in paper money rose daily, and, when a Robert Morris ship arrived in the harbor and failed to unload its cargo, Thomas Paine howled that Morris was provoking inflation by creating artificial shortages. As one Morris critic put it crudely, Morris was "getting rich by sucking the blood of this country.[81]

As it turned out, Morris did not own or have any control over the cargo in question. The actual owners had chartered the Morris ship to carry cargo to their Philadelphia agent, and it was he who had ordered the cargo withheld to take advantage of rising prices, thus vindicating Morris.

As summer progressed, however, runaway inflation made it difficult, often impossible, for working class families and militiamen to feed their families. Angered by open displays of lavish merchant spending at taverns and clubs, the workers and soldiers formed mobs and marched in the streets demanding price controls. Morris and other merchants replied just as forcefully that price controls would reduce business profits, force shops to close and discharge hundreds of their workers.

"Trade should be as free as air," the editor of the *Pennsylvania Packet* argued, "uninterrupted as the tide, and though it will be sometimes high at one place and low at another, yet it will ever return of itself sufficiently near to a proper level."[82]

Early in October, a mob of protesters seized four merchants, forcibly marching them along Philadelphia's streets. Cries erupted: "Get Wilson," they shouted, referring to the prominent lawyer and close friend of Robert Morris and other Philadelphia merchants.

Although Morris had discredited charges that he had withheld goods from the market by refusing to unload a ship, the mob chased Morris and his merchant friends from their Coffee House seats to Wilson's house. With shotguns and rifles in hand, Morris and the others—skilled hunters all—took positions at every window and fired at the approaching mob. Five attackers fell with the first volley. Several more fell trying to break through a rear door.

Morris, meanwhile, had sent a message for help to Pennsylvania President [i.e., governor] Joseph Reed, who had served with Morris in the Continental Congress and responded quickly by sending the city cavalry to crush the attack. Morris and his band had killed four attackers and wounded fourteen at what became known as "Fort Wilson." Reed's troop took 27 prisoners and scattered the rest.

Although the shooting had stopped, the bitterness persisted and threatened to explode into full-scale class warfare on Philadelphia's streets. Morris sent Mary and his children to the safety of his rebuilt mansion at "The Hills." By then they boasted five children: Maria had been born the previous April. By then, their oldest boy Robert III was 10, Thomas 8, William White 7, and Hester 5.

As the militants regrouped for a second, more serious attack, Morris urged Wilson to flee the state. "Retreat until the ferment is over," he counseled. "In the present state of

things, the passions of men might do you injustice that their own judgments would hereafter...regret."[83]

Henry Laurens warned of another imminent revolution. "We are at this moment on a precipice," he wrote to John Adams. "What I have long dreaded...seems now to be breaking forth—a convulsion among the people."[84]

Robert Morris went to his pier, armed his loyal employees, and prepared to fight, even die, protecting his property against approaching mobs.

Chapter 6

THE BITE OF THE SLUM DOG

A

lthough Philadelphia remained tense after the Fort Wilson fracas, the approach of winter weather cooled temperatures on both sides. Voters removed Morris and other merchants from the state assembly, ending the heated debates over changing the state constitution. At the same time, rebuilding Philadelphia created enough jobs and money to calm tempers of disgruntled working men and keep them and the merchants far enough apart from each other to avoid further conflicts.

Relieved of government responsibilities, Morris turned his full attention to making money, and he made it as never before. As one historian put it later—somewhat speciously and perhaps maliciously: "The idea that Robert Morris financed the Revolution out of his own pocket is purely mythological. The truth is that the Revolution financed Robert Morris."[85]

Although Morris emerged from the Revolution a rich man, he had in fact proved a staunch patriot, risking his life and indeed his last penny for the Revolution and his friend George Washington. He had paid, from his own pocket, the troops of the Continental Army and, indeed, exhausted his financial assets. That he had the savvy, courage, and luck to invest his remaining assets wisely and rebuild his fortune by war's end does not diminish his sacrifices or transform them into myth.

Just as prosperity returned to Philadelphia, however, the fortunes of war inflicted sharp losses on other parts of the nation. At the end of 1778, Savannah, Georgia, and its strategic port facilities, fell to the British, with Augusta falling the following year, along with Portsmouth and Newport, Virginia.

In New Jersey, meanwhile, the coldest winter in more than a century had frozen the waters surrounding Manhattan Island and left Washington and his troops encamped at Morristown, New Jersey, in worse conditions than they had experienced at Valley Forge. Washington called the situation "alarming," with troops "on half allowance and not more than three days bread on hand, nor anywhere within reach.... Our magazines are absolutely empty," he pleaded with Pennsylvania President Reed, "and our commissaries entirely destitute of money." Washington predicted "the army will infallibly disband in a fortnight."[86]

With Congress out of money, Robert Morris—now a private citizen—stepped in, writing to everyone in his network of merchants to raise funds for Congress.

"I think every well-wisher to the country should make it a point to supply them."[87]

After one merchant-trader replied that one of his ships had arrived in port carrying ninety tons of lead ballast. Morris "secured the lead...set more than one hundred people to work during the night. Before morning a supply of cartridges was ready and sent off to the army."[88]

Morris was unable, however, to help Congress stem the free-fall of the Continental dollar, and in March 1780, when it fell to near zero, Congress had no choice but to replace it with a new U.S. dollar and recall the continentals at a rate of forty to one. Then, with the fall of Charleston, even the value of the new dollar plunged.

Again, Robert Morris had to save the Revolution by coaxing—bullying is more accurate—Philadelphia's merchants to contribute more than 100,000 of the new dollars and an additional £400 to buy flour and foodstuffs for the troops. They knew they had little choice but comply if they wanted to continue doing business with the powerful Morris company.

Mary Morris, meanwhile, organized her friends to supplement her husband's efforts and raised almost as much as her husband had. Her appeals only casually hinted a promise of invitations to receptions and dinners at her elegant home.

The two Morrises provoked so great a flow of funds that Morris had to expand his business enterprise and organize what was the nation's first bank to receive the funds. Far from the rapacious capitalist portrayed by foes of capitalism, Morris simply identified public needs and established businesses to fill those needs—at a reasonable profit. In doing so he created what was and remains the foundation of American capitalism.

Called the Pennsylvania Bank, the pioneering Morris bank differed substantially from today's conventional banks in that it was merely a money warehouse from which to disburse funds to the American military. When it opened, depositors initially invested a total of £300,000 in interest-bearing notes redeemable in six months with interest. It was unconventional in that it did not offer account holders the right to withdraw funds at will. The bank nonetheless won the support of Congress, which pledged the full faith of the United States government to guarantee depositors against losses.

By mid-year, the Morris bank had become the primary source of funds for Washington's army. As he had before, Morris had again rescued the American Revolution, and, by summer's end, Pennsylvanians hailed Morris by returning him to the Assembly

Seventeen-seventy-nine ended badly, however, and the new year boded worse when the once-trusted and heroic Brigadier General Benedict Arnold committed treason by feeding military information to the British. Arnold had previously been stripped of his command in Philadelphia for incompetence and sent instead to head the isolated Hudson River fort at West Point. Angry about his loss of stature, he delivered detailed plans of the fort for money and an appointment in the British as a brigadier general.

Arnold's defection left Washington's officer corps in disarray and demoralized. Officers of all ranks eyed each other suspiciously, questioning each other's decisions. Distrust of officers among the rank and file erupted into mutinies.

On January 1, 1781, 2,400 Continental Army veterans in the Pennsylvania Line, some unpaid for as many as three years, seized company arms and ammunition, fired at and wounded several officers, then, led by their sergeants, marched toward Philadelphia to force Congress at bayonet point to pay them their due. Congress fled to Princeton, New Jersey, and Washington ordered a battalion from West Point to crush the mutiny.

With Congress bankrupt, however, all eyes again turned to Robert Morris, the man they now routinely called "The Financier. Still the fervent patriot with unlimited business skills and, apparently, bottomless pockets, Morris had already worked so many financial miracles that most members of Congress assumed he could and would continue producing what Washington called "magick money." But the mutinies and the inaction and flight by Congress had infuriated both Morris and Washington.

"There is such a combination of circumstances to exhaust the patience of the soldiery that it begins at length to be worn out," Washington barked at Pennsylvania President Reed, his former aide de camp. "We see in every line of the army the most serious features of mutiny and sedition...and unless a system very different from that which has prevailed be immediately adopted throughout the states, our affairs must soon become desperate beyond the possibility of recovery."[89]

By 1781, Congress had issued just under 200 million in new dollars, while military quartermasters had issued another $50 million in paper certificates for supplies. The value of both plunged, provoking a fierce, albeit private, scolding by Morris to try to force the states to ratify the Articles of Confederation and convert themselves into the semblance of a nation. At his insistence, it then withdrew 120 million from the marketplace to give the nation the semblance of fiscal responsibility.

Ironically, the war that had bankrupted Congress had poured endless profits into the pockets of many of its members and the oligarchs who controlled state governments. Although British blockades and privateers had intercepted some waterborne traffic of American agricultural goods, the shortages that followed sent prices rising and increased profits from shiploads that did reach their destinations.

American growers produced crops almost cost-free with slave labor in the middle-Atlantic and southern states and unpaid indentured workers in the north. Although Washington recognized that the government was "deeply in debt," he argued correctly that "the nation is rich and their riches can afford a fund which will not be easily exhausted."[90]

When the Revolution began, Congress had boasted of the nation's wealth, convincing the world it would be the government of a new, rich nation of *united* states.

With the Declaration of Independence bearing the signature of Robert Morris, who had stuffed sacks of gold coins in every vault he could find in Europe and America, Congress had had no difficulty floating nearly $40 million worth of paper overseas and borrowing more than $20 million from wealthy investors. Along with foreign government leaders, investors assumed they were lending money to a responsible new national government backed not only by the nation's wealthiest man, but by an oligarchy of wealthy plantation-owners who ruled the entire South and dominated Congress.

"The creditors trust the union," Morris had declared, insisting that the strength of the states "is derived from their union."[91]

But there was no union—no "United States of America." It did not exist and never had. Nor had the Declaration of Independence contained a word or hint of a new nation. Indeed, five years would elapse before the states reluctantly approved the Articles of Confederation, which, far from creating a union, had created only "a league of friendship." The Articles left each state sovereign and independent, with "every power, jurisdiction, and right" it had before signing the Articles, and, in contrast to the Declaration of Independence, the Articles incited bitter debate over state sovereignty among state leaders.

Even as troops from multiple states fought under a single military banner, their political leaders rejected even the most fragile political ties to each other and left the Continental Congress an impotent debating society that became a laughingstock among nations and the object of loathing among bedraggled American troops, who adjudged it a den of thieves.

As the debate over granting powers to a federal government grew more bitter, Robert Morris warned that "everything which injures the union must impair the strength which is dependent upon it.... Nothing therefore ought to prevent the free and generous communication of all necessary powers to Congress."[92]

With each of Washington's call for funds for his troops, Morris and a handful of his supporters in Congress renewed their calls for a stronger union. With Washington demanding more money in the winter if 1781, Morris called on Congress to comply by imposing taxes. His proposal met with a chorus of catcalls and shouts. Delegates shouted that the sole purpose of the revolution had been to end government taxation, not restore it. Washington immediately jumped into the debate to support his friend:

"Unless a system very different from that which has for a long time prevailed be immediately adopted throughout the states," Washington warned, "our affairs must soon become desperate beyond the point of recovery.... The crisis in every point of view is extraordinary and extraordinary expedients are necessary."[93]

Moved by Washington's plea, even Thomas Paine—a staunch opponent of taxation when the war began—issued a pamphlet that compared wartime taxes and populations in England and America and embarrassed opponents of taxation. England, he pointed out, collected £1.13s.3d per personeach year from its population of seven million to cover annual expenses of war and government.

In contrast, the war was costing three million Americans a mere thirteen shillings and four pence per person—a pittance so far from burdensome that he urged Congress to impose import duties immediately and called on states to impose income and property taxes.

While Joseph Reed held army mutineers in check at Philadelphia, that mutiny prompted a similar mutiny by the New Jersey line in Pompton, New Jersey, to the north. Fearful of an epidemic of mutinies, Washington acted swiftly, sending troops to crush the New Jersey mutineers and execute their two leaders—both of them sergeants.

The violence in the military left state leaders so shaken that they yielded to the persistent Morris demands to strengthen the central government. On February 2, 1781, Maryland became the last of the thirteen states to ratify the "Articles of Confederation and perpetual union" creating—in name at least—"The United States of America."

Congress immediately streamlined its operation methods, replacing unruly committees of legislators with individual heads to administer the principle departments: war, marine, treasury, and foreign affairs.

On February 20, 1781, Congress unanimously elected Robert Morris—Superintendent of Finance[94] to head the new Department of Treasury, granting him "all the powers, privileges, authorities, and emoluments" of the office. Although Morris had served as de facto head of the Treasury since the beginning of the Revolution, he had only chaired a committee for part of that time. It bore the same name as the post he had held previously and in which he had usurped powers in the absence of Congress, but the new post specified his powers as the previous appointment had not. In effect, it was to make him the young nation's first true executive.

As delegates stood to applaud their new appointee, however, Morris shocked them all by remaining seated, staring ahead glumly, without as much as a smile or nod to acknowledge his appointment. As the applause died and silence enveloped the chamber; the president had no choice but adjourn the session, and the delegates shuffled out, leaving Morris alone with his thoughts.

Although Morris, like most delegates, believed his new office was essential to creating a stronger central government, he did not want the job. After a stressful life of more than twenty years in international trade—working the docks, toiling in the counting house, sailing the seas as a cargo master—and after six equally stressful years in public service unofficially serving in the very post that Congress had now officially granted him, Morris was exhausted. He had looked forward to a life of repose in his luxurious Philadelphia mansion and country estates with his beautiful wife and now six children.

The arrival of French General Rochambeau with 5,000 French troops gave Washington a numerical advantage in manpower and firing power that seemed all but certain to end the war and bring peace to America. And Morris wanted nothing more than peace—on the fields of battle, of course, but also at home, with his beloved wife and family and his cellar-full of French wines.

"This appointment," he raged in his diary on February 21, the day after Congress had appointed him, "was evidently contrary to my private interest and if accepted must deprive me of those enjoyments social and domestic which my time of life required and which my circumstances entitled me to, and as a vigorous execution of my duties must inevitably expose me to the resentment of disappointed and designing men and to the calumny and detraction of the envious and malicious. I was therefore absolutely determined not to engage in so arduous an undertaking."[95]

Leaders across the land, however, pleaded with him to accept the post, with his young friend Lt. Col. Alexander Hamilton, a top aide to General Washington, arguing that only his acceptance of the post would ensure American independence.

"'Tis by introducing order into our finances by restoring public credit—not by gaining battles—that we are finally to gain our object," Hamilton wrote. "You may render America and the world no less a service than the establishment of American independence. In the frankness of truth, Sir, I believe you are the Man best capable of performing this great work."[96]

But Benjamin Franklin sent Morris a personal note from Paris, warning that "the business you have undertaken is of so complex a nature and must engross so much of your time and attention as necessarily to hurt your private interests...while you are sure of being censured by malevolent critics...who will abuse you while you are serving them and wound your character in nameless pamphlets, thereby resembling those little dirty stinking insects that attack us only in the dark."[97]

It was the self-effacing John Swanwick in the Morris counting house, however, who settled the matter for Morris. By then, he had become Morris's most trusted aide.

"The safety and glory of the United States are involved in your acceptance or refusal," Swanwick pleaded. "My opinion [is] that the fate of this country is so nearly tied to yours that as she rises and falls so is your fate determined.... If order be not established in the money matters of America" it would mean "the ruin of yourself and this country.

"I declare to you, sir, most solemnly...that I do not believe there is in America any man fit for this office of Financier but you."

Swanwick went on to list the essential characteristics for anyone assuming the post, among them, "*fortune* [his italics], that he be not subservient to temptation of wealth...*abilities*, that he do no injury to the country by neglect or ignorance...*a man of weight abroad*...accustomed to rank and honors, not a man indebted for them."

Swanwick then apologized for "forgetting his station" and having the audacity to advise so honored a personage as his employer. He said he looked to Morris as a father figure and prayed that "history shall not forget you, and the day on which America so eminently showed her affection for you shall be forever the most happy on her records."[98]

Deeply moved by Swanwick's words, Morris finally responded to Congress. On May 14, three months after the appointment, he said he would accept the post, but only on his own terms. He expressed appreciation to Congress "for the honor done me" and its "strong mark of confidence," but added: "After twenty years of assiduous application to business as a merchant, I find myself at that period where my mind, body, and inclination combine to make me seek relaxation and ease." Assumption of the appointment as superintendent of finance, he said, would mean "a sacrifice of that ease, of much social and domestic enjoyment, and of very material interests."

He said he had taken an active part in "the contest we are engaged in" when it appeared to him "just and necessary. As it became more dangerous, I...was stimulated to the greatest exertions in my power." Although he acknowledged "the want of arrangement in our moneyed affairs," the arrival of the French army had changed the complexion of the military situation, and he said he would accept appointment as Superintendent of Finance only under conditions he believed—and perhaps hoped—might force Congress to reconsider his appointment.

"I am bound in honor and by contracts to support...certain commercial establishments... If therefore...the Office of Superintendent of Finance is incompatible with commercial concerns and connections...I cannot on any consideration consent to violate [these] engagements."

In other words, Morris said he would not cut his business ties—and with good reason. Even George Washington had maintained full control of his enormous agricultural enterprise at Mount Vernon during the entire war. Having appointed his cousin Lund Washington to supervise the plantation, General Washington left almost nothing to chance–or to Lund Washington's discretion during the war.

"If you could exchange the old greys for young mares, it would be a good way of getting quit of them," Washington wrote from the banks of the Delaware River in 1776 after his humiliating defeat in New York and retreat across New Jersey.

"If you can get a good match for the stallion, I should like it very well—but let the match be good & the horse handsome.... I desire you to plant locusts across from the new garden to the spinning house...as also at the other wall from the old garden gate to the smoke house and hen house...."[99]

In addition to retaining his business connections, Morris demanded complete control over hiring and firing in his office. "I think it indispensably necessary that the appointment of all persons who are to act in my office...should be made by myself," he declared, along with "*absolute power* [his italics] of dismissing...all persons whatever.... The determination of Congress thereon will enable me to determine whether to accept or decline the appointment."

He also insisted that Congress assume all responsibility for its existing debts and limit his responsibility to oversight of government finances after his assumption of his new office.

He then added that he hoped his demands would force Congress to withdraw its nomination: "I must observe that the Act of Congress...describing the duties of the Superintendent of Finance requires the execution of many things for which adequate powers are not provided, and it cannot be expected that your officer can in such cases be responsible. These however, may be the subjects of future discussion."[100]

In effect, Morris all but refused to accept the appointment if Congress did not grant him *absolute* powers.

A week after receiving Morris's reply, Congress debated his demands, expressing strong reservations about his insistence on retaining all his business connections. In the end. Congres yielded to all his demands.

On May 14, Morris accepted the post, promising only "honest industry." Intent on establishing cordial if not warm relations with Congress, Morris sent the delegates a peace offering conceding that "the great magnitude" of the task he faced would require "my whole time, study, and attention" and that if he continued operating his own business, he might "give rise to illiberal reflections equally painful to me and injurious to the public." He then announced his intention to put "the accounts of my private business...into the hands of other persons.

> In accepting the office bestowed on me, I sacrifice much of my interest, my ease, my domestic enjoyments and internal tranquility. If I know my own heart, I make these sacrifices with a disinterested view to the service of my country. I am ready to go still further: the United States may command everything I have except my integrity.[101]

Although Franklin had warned Morris of the dangers inherent in the new post, he nonetheless heaped compliments on Morris for his previous services to the new nation and promised "every assistance that my situation here [in Paris]...may enable me to afford you.... For besides my affection for the glorious cause we are both engaged in, I value myself upon your friendship and shall be happy if mine can be made of any use to you."[102]

Washington was even more elated, pledging, "My hand and heart shall be with you. And, as far as my assistance will or can go, command it."

In a rare emotional outpouring, Washington promised Morris, "I will aid your endeavors to the extent of my abilities and with all the powers I am vested. I shall be happy in a meeting with you and would have wrote [sic] you more fully...if the bearer was not waiting. I could not however, refrain from embracing the first opportunity of expressing the pleasure I get at hearing...that you had entered upon the duties of your office and to assure you with how much truth and sincerity I am Dear Sir your Most Obedient and Affectionate Servant."[103]

As Washington wrote to Morris, hungry unpaid Pennsylvania troops renewed their mutiny. Washington responded harshly, crushing the disturbances with loyal troops and executing several of the mutineers.

"A committee of Congress called on me with a letter from his Excellency Gen. Washington," Morris scribbled in his diary, "showing the distress of the army for want of bread and... empowering Genl. Washington to seize flour...wherever he could find it. I determined to procure supplies and pledge my private credit."[104] Just as Washington had seized direct control of army operations in the wake of the Conway Cabal, Morris now took direct control of army procurement and finances, bypassing Congress and state governments.

"A committee of Congress having communicated to me the distress of your army for want of bread," Morris wrote to Washington on May 29, 1781, "I found myself immediately impressed with the strongest desire to afford you relief.... I have wrote to [Albany, N.Y., merchant/banker] Major Genl. Schuyler and to [New Jersey merchant] Thomas Lowrey...requesting their immediate exertions to procure upon their own credit 1000 barrels of flour each to send...to camp deliverable to your Excellency's order, and I have pledged to pay them in hard money."

Left unsaid was the heavy-handed pressure Morris could exert on individual merchants such as Schuyler and Lowrey. They and most other merchants had taken full advantage of Army shortages to hoard supplies and command higher prices. Morris acted to break their collective financial backs. Had they not complied, they would have suffered the crushing bite of the slum dog: A break in a key vendor's supply lines via the Morris pipelines, for example, or a long payment delay by a major customer—i.e., Morris himself or one of his subsidiaries.

None dared ignore Morris "requests"—not Schuyler, not Lowrey.

"As an occasion has turned up for you to show your activity and attention to the interest and service of your country," Morris wrote not too subtly to Lowrey, "I must therefore request that you will use your best skill, judgment, and industry in purchasing on the lowest terms you can one thousand barrels of sound, sweet flour and in sending it to camp in the most expeditious and least expensive manner that you can contrive. You understand business too well not to think of sending it forward...as fast as you can get it. You will also no doubt seek to procure this quantity as near to the camp as it can be got in order to lessen charges of transportation."[105]

He was equally blunt with Schuyler: "General Washington is distressed for want of an immediate supply of flour.... I must therefore request that you will take the most speedy and effectual measures to deliver....1000 barrels of flour which I am sure you will purchase and cause to be transported on the most reasonable terms that are practicable. No time must be lost."[106]

To end corrupt practices in the handling of army supplies, Morris ordered deliveries made directly to Washington instead of the commissaries "because there are many assertions made...that provisions are not delivered." Indeed, non-delivery of supplies by quartermasters and their staffs—not shortages of foodstuffs—had caused the near-starvation of troops at Valley Forge in the winter of 1777-1778. Instead of transporting foodstuffs to camp, the quartermaster general at the time had ordered everything sold to merchants in nearby

Philadelphia. When Washington discovered what was happening he demoted the quartermaster-general and relieved him of his duties.

"Perhaps it would be time well spent to appoint an officer to attend to receipt and delivery of this flour," Morris advised Washington. "I desired...the weights marked on the head of every barrel in order that proper account might be easily taken thereof.... We must introduce the strictest economy into the issuing departments or the army will forever be exposed to wants which are not less disgraceful than painful."[107]

Morris told Washington that he had been on the verge of refusing the appointment as Superintendent of Finance because of the harsh criticism Thomas Paine and others had heaped on him for his earlier efforts building America's munitions trade.

"Contrary to my inclination," he wrote, "I consented to make another attempt in favor of this poor distressed country...inspired [by] your bright example.... I promise assiduity in the pursuit of honest measures and an economical expenditure of it.... I must rely on the best information, intelligence, assistance, and advice I can procure from you.... I would hope that a free, candid, sincere communication may take place between us; much confidential intercourse must ensue."[108]

Within days, the "confidential intercourse" Morris had sought got under way, with Morris confiding in Washington that victory would be impossible without repeal of tender laws allowing states to print paper money, which had created a confusing patchwork of state and Confederation currencies.

He said he wanted Congress to establish a national bank, comparable to the Bank of England, run by the central government. Once established, it would then introduce a single, national currency to replace all paper currencies then in circulation.

"I am also pressing...to levy effective taxes in hard currency," he told Washington, "for my objects are to reduce public expenditures...and to obtain revenues...to meet those expenses as nearly as can be."

Morris then added waggishly, "I have the pleasure to hear that Mr. Lowrey has sent 1000 barrels of flour to camp."[109]

A few days later, Morris extracted a better price from Lowrey and boasted to Washington, "I thought proper to agree with him for 1000 barrels more, fresh and sweet, to be delivered to Your Excellency's order."[110]

Washington was ecstatic with the Morris proposals. Abandoning his usually austere tone, he told Morris his proposals "afforded me infinite satisfaction, as the measures you are pursuing for subsisting the Army accord with my ideas [in contrast to the] small degree [with which] the requisitions of Congress had been complied with."[111]

By early July, Morris had worked another miracle, having sent market prices for foodstuffs plunging. Just as he had used his own trading network to bid prices up in peacetime, he now sent prices spiraling downward by ordering merchant partners in different regions to dump enough supplies on the market to undermine the prices demanded by hoarders. Even the largest merchant knew better than to defy Morris and his trading behemoth.

"You mention to have been written by Genl. Schuyler respecting a greater supply of flour than he expected," Morris wrote facetiously to Washington from Philadelphia. "Flour remains so plenty that there has not been a day in which I could not buy 5,000 to 10,000 barrels in this city, and the price has fallen from 28/ and 30/ to 17/ but I think 15/ will buy 112 pounds very soon." Morris promised Washington that "you cannot want provisions so long as I can find money to pay for them."[112]

Morris's barely concealed manipulation of market prices quickly forced the last of the hoarders to release supplies, and speculators soon abandoned food markets.

The merchants and speculators serving in Congress and state assemblies recognized they were no match for Robert Morris, and, on

July 5, 1781, he was able to write to Washington that Congress had passed an act vesting Morris "with powers to dispose of the specific supplies required from the several states [according to] your Excellency's advice [as] will best promote the public interest and the purposes of the present campaign."[113]

Morris had less success forcing state governors to comply with requisitions of Congress for money, however. "I must urge the most speedy and punctual compliance," he wrote in a circular letter to which none of the states replied, let alone complied. Morris was not their Superintendent of Finance; they had given him no authority over their money.[114]

As Morris wrote, General Comte de Rochambeau was leading his 5,000-man French army from Rhode Island, across Connecticut to rendezvous with Washington's 6,000 troops north of New York. At an earlier meeting, the two generals had planned a joint assault on the central British encampment on New York Island [Manhattan].

On August 2, however, Washington wrote asking Morris to come to the Washington encampment immediately. When Morris arrived, Washington said he had changed his plan, explaining that with the Franco-American army just to its north, the British would almost certainly reinforce New York and weaken the force left behind in Virginia. Virginia, rather than New York, therefore, would be "the next object which ought to engage our attention."[115]

Washington said he would leave a token force in New Jersey to keep the British in New York on guard, but would lead most of the Franco-American force southward to Virginia. A French fleet from the Caribbean, he said, was already sailing towards Chesapeake Bay to trap Cornwallis on the cape at Yorktown and prevent escape by water.

"I am not without hopes...to carry a body of men...by water," Washington told Morris, hoping to get the army to Virginia by the fastest means—namely, by water southward on Chesapeake Bay—and spare his men a long debilitating overland trek.

> What I would wish you to inform yourself of...is what number of tons of shipping could be obtained in Philadelphia at any time between this and the 20th of this month [August] and whether there could be obtained...a few deep-waisted sloops and schooners to carry horses. The number of double-decked vessels which may be wanted, of 200 tons and upwards, will not exceed thirty..... You will oblige me by giving me your opinion of the number of vessels which might be obtained at Baltimore or other places in Chesapeake in the time mentioned.[116]

Morris set to work feverishly stockpiling goods and military equipment. To support his effort, Congress named him Agent of Marine on September 7, with powers of a secretary of the navy to "direct, fit out, equip, and employ" all American naval vessels "in such manner as shall appear to him best calculated to promote the interests of these United States."[117]

But the failure of Congress to establish the central bank Morris had demanded had left the government and its new Agent of Marine without funds to finance his huge mission. Hoping to perform another financial miracle, Morris again contacted every governor demanding compliance in the demands of Congress for money.

"We shall furnish much to the Southern Army," the governor of North Carolina replied disingenuously, before providing "money for the United States."[118] New York's reply indicated that it might supply 3,000 barrels of flour, but qualified its contribution as "probable not absolutely certain."[119]

When other governors failed to respond, Morris sent them another circular letter on July 16, listing the requisitions for each state: New Hampshire nearly $7 million, Connecticut nearly $24 million, New York nearly $12.5 million, Pennsylvania more than $38.5 million, Delaware nearly $2.4 million, and Virginia nearly $34.5 million.

No sooner had he sent the circular letter than Washington stunned him by announcing that for the expedition to proceed, "it will be necessary to give the American troops destined for southern service one month's pay in specie"—in advance![120]

With that, Morris all but despaired. He had exhausted his own funds and virtually all his credit and, with British warships blockading transatlantic traffic to and from America, he could no longer access any of his own or his company's funds overseas. By then, too, the Arnold defection and troop mutinies had eroded much of the will of some state assemblies to continue the fight, and Congress no longer had any funds to do so. America's financial miracle maker warned Washington that his expedition to Yorktown was doomed to fail before it could even get under way. Grim-faced, Washington thought for a while, then turned to Morris and issued a simple command: "Send for Solomon."

Chapter 7

ART MAGICK

I n the spring of 1781, George Washington developed a scheme to combine his Continental Army with the 5,000-man French army and, with the powerful French navy offshore, dislodge the British from New York. He changed his mind abruptly, however, after French Admiral Joseph Paul, Comte de Grasse sent word that his Caribbean fleet with 3,000 French troops aboard would be available for action only in the Chesapeake Bay area from mid-August until late October.

Washington then met with French General Jean Baptiste Donatien de Vimeur Comte de Rochambeau to plan a massive, Franco-American assault against the British in Virginia. He called on Robert Morris to order and stockpile the necessary goods and military equipment.

As Morris went to work, the purchasing power of government-issued money fell again and left American troops ready to desert unless they received their pay in specie (gold or silver), or a form of currency with equivalent value. In addition to back pay owed to many, all demanded a month's pay in advance before embarking on the Virginia campaign with its risks of being stranded far from home.

As he had done once before, Morris replaced worthless currency with printed Morris notes, which mimicked government currency and were backed by his personal credit, "which thank heaven I have preserved through all the tempests of the war."[121] At the time, every banker, business man, and merchant of consequence in the western world knew his name and held a share of his wealth, directly or indirectly. But Morris had, in fact, spent every last penny he owned. Sheer pretense and bluster underlay the preservation of his personal credit.

When, therefore, Morris told his friend the general that he had exhausted his funds and could not cover more Morris notes with cash, Washington blanched, thought for a moment, then snapped, "Send for Haym Solomon!"

A Jewish refugee-turned-currency-broker from Poland, Haym Solomon had become a fervent patriot after arriving in America in 1772. He had joined New York's Sons of Liberty, then served as a spy for Washington before lighting the flames that had engulfed British headquarters and most of lower Manhattan island in September 1776. Imprisoned by the British and sentenced to die, he escaped and fled to Philadelphia, where his command of seven languages allowed him to establish a brokerage of sorts for members of Congress, converting their funds into acceptable currencies.

Following Washington's instructions, Morris met with Solomon, who immediately sold foreign exchange certificates[122] worth $20 million. Morris and Solomon then arranged for a shipment of $470,000 in French silver coins to back up the Morris notes given to the troops. Then, with the malfeasance at Valley Forge still fresh in his memory, Morris agreed to serve as Washington's quartermaster on the Virginia campaign to ensure that every penny spent would put food, drink, and ammunition in the hands of American troops.

With pockets filled and bellies satiated when summer of 1781 ended, the troops began the march to Maryland's north shore, where they boarded ships that Morris had procured and sailed down Chesapeake Bay to storm British defenses at Yorktown. After three days, the British surrendered. Washington had produced a military miracle, facilitated by the financial miracle produced by a Polish Jew, Haym Solomon, and the Anglican slum dog, Robert Morris. The two miracles would prove the beginning of the end of one great empire and the end of the beginning for another.

Yorktown was the last great battle of the American War of Independence. The capture of an entire British army at Yorktown ended British hopes for victory, while subsequent losses to the French in the Caribbean forced the House of Commons to sue for peace in the Americas. Anglo-American peace talks began in the spring of 1782, French forces returned to France on Christmas Eve of that year, and all sides agreed to peace in January 1783. On November 25, 1783, the last British troops sailed from New York and left the United States.

Victory at Yorktown allowed Robert Morris to return to his family and his business in Philadelphia. As buyers on both sides of the Atlantic began compensating for wartime shortages, Morris coffers filled to overflowing, allowing him to buy and renovate a stunning three story brick mansion thought to be Philadelphia's largest. Three stories tall at 190 High Street (later Market Street at Sixth), it stood in the center of the city only two blocks from the State House and had once been the home of colonial governor Richard Penn. By then, the Morris household swarmed with children—six altogether: Robert Morris III, 11; Thomas, 10; William White, 9; Hester Marshall, 7; Charles 4; and Maria Nixon, 2. [The Morrises would have one more child, Henry, in July 1784.]

In addition to vast renovations, Morris installed a modern kitchen, an ice house, a bath house, and stables for twelve horses. The central part of the house boasted two dining rooms—one for entertaining (at a dozen tables topped with twelve dozen wine glasses) and a drawing room 'brilliant beyond anything you could imagine."

An invitation to the Morris home to a dinner or ball soon became Philadelphia's highest social honor.

The Morrises reserved that part of the house with the second dining room for the family. It had six bedrooms and quarters for the household staff. Morris also refurbished his property at The Hills, expanding it to 300 acres and adding a substantial brick home for his caretaker.

Although life at the Morris home soon returned to its pre-Revolution splendor, conditions in many parts of the nation deteriorated because of what Morris assailed as "financial mob rule." While British, American, and French diplomats were negotiating peace terms in Paris in 1782, Washington's army had encamped in Newburgh, N.Y., 70 miles north of New York, to await the signing of a peace treaty and the war's official end. State assemblies, however, balked at paying and feeding an idle army, and officers and troops threatened another mutiny.

Always ready to respond to Washington's summonses for help, Morris settled on a bold move that met the army's demands and, coincidentally, spurred the growth of American free enterprise: he organized the founding of the nation's first incorporated national bank.

Calling it the Bank of North America, Morris funded it privately by issuing 1,000 shares for sale at $400 each—$400,000 in all. He bought 633 shares for the government with $250,000 from a French government loan, creating a hybrid institution—both a private *and* government bank—warehousing government funds but subject to no government or other oversight but his own.

With all sides agreed on a formal peace treaty, the last of the 100,000 American loyalists sailed from New York in April 1783, and, except for small standby forces, most of the American army disbanded. Morris turned his attention from paying troops to reforming government finances. He faced an impossible task.

The end of the war had ended any pretense of unity in the Confederation Congress, and, given the power of any single member-state to veto any change in rules, the Morris fiscal reforms met with nothing but rejection. Morris was able to introduce a system of competitive bidding for government contracts, but he met with angry refusals when he proposed building a government mint along with a plan to convert American money to a decimal currency.

Congress went on to reject all the rest of his proposed reforms: mandatory financing of Confederation government operations; the maintenance of standby military forces to repel Indian attacks on the frontier and repel invasions by foreign armies; an impost law giving the bankrupt Confederation government authority to levy duties on imports.

When Congress rejected the last of his proposals—the impost—a group of nearly 300 infuriated soldiers, their bayonets fixed, marched on Philadelphia's State House (now Independence Hall) demanding overdue back pay.

Congress fled Philadelphia to the safety of nearby Princeton, New Jersey.

After it reconvened, Congress avenged its humiliation by all-but-firing the entire army. Arguing that the Atlantic Ocean would provide America with adequate protection against foreign attacks, it reduced army size from 11,000 men to 2,000. On December 23, 1783, George Washington resigned as commander in chief of the Army, and, by 1785, Congress had disbanded the Navy and reduced the Army to only 625 soldiers.

"How long is a nation who will do nothing itself to rely on the aid of others?" Morris asked as he pleaded for funds to pay the troops. "How long will one part of a community bear the burdens of the whole? How long will an Army undergo want in the midst of plenty?" Morris warned that, without financial reforms, the next military threat to American independence will "sweep away our feeble confederation and endanger, if not overturn, the union of these states."

Morris then developed a proposal that proved far too difficult to understand for the ill-schooled, though wealthy, planters and tradesmen who peopled Congress.

In effect, Morris called for establishing capitalism as the foundation of the United States economy by "funding the debt" that Congress and the states had accumulated during the Revolution.

In effect, the national government would assume all such debts and float long-term bonds to create a perpetual *capital* fund to wipe out war debts, rebuild the military, and invest in capital projects such as building roads and canals—all at the same time. Morris foresaw nothing less than a capitalist nation, with public and private spending based on long-term capital debt.

The majority of delegates could not conceive of paying debts by going deeper into debt and charged Morris with scheming to enrich himself. Only New York lawyer Alexander Hamilton defended Morris. A close aide to Washington during the war and a heroic leader at Yorktown, Hamilton had married into New York's Schuyler banking family and had studied economics at King's College (later Columbia University), but he stood alone in urging adoption of the Morris proposal to fund the debt.

As hoots filled the hall, Congress all but shouted another rejection at Morris, who threw up his hands in despair and resigned.

Calling fiscal reform "the last essential work of our glorious Revolution," he said he had planned to continue "to sacrifice Time, Property, and domestic Bliss" and remain at his post if Congress had enacted a permanent provision for handling public debts.

"To increase our Debts while the Prospect of paying them diminishes does not consist [conform] with my ideas of Integrity," he declared. " I must therefore quit a situation which becomes utterly insupportable."[123]

With Morris and his annoying calls for fiscal responsibility out of earshot, the voices of unreasonable partisanship filled the hall of Congress. Members divided between those favoring state supremacy and those favoring union, with only the latter willing to flirt with funding the debt. Those opposed to funding were a solid majority and easily outvoted supporters of the Morris plan. Talk of funding the debt all but ended.

With Yorktown fading from American memories, costs of public services for which British authorities had paid when they ruled the colonies began to bleed state treasuries. By spring 1786, a punitive 10% limit Britain had placed on imports from her former American colonies had turned America's economic slump into a depression. Imports from Britain dropped 30 percent, exports 6 percent. American farm revenues plunged 20 percent and tax delinquencies soared, along with property confiscations for nonpayment of state property taxes.

Although American merchants were free to trade anywhere in the world—as they had not been permitted to do under British rule—the rest of the world's lack of familiarity with American products and American currencies made such trade difficult, and American traders were unable to compensate for the decline of income from Britain.

Always alert for new profit opportunities, however, Morris pioneered hitherto nonexistent American trade with Asia by buying a half-share with savvy European traders in the *Empress of China*. His investment soon opened a lucrative new trading relationship with China, with Chinese tea and silks, formerly bought from English exporters flowing directly to Morris in America, free of costly British duties.

Even more profitable was the Morris trade with France, where tobacco had become a national passion—especially snuff, or "smokeless tobacco" made from ground or pulverized tobacco leaves.

Through a series of secret contracts, Morris established a near monopoly, becoming the largest buyer of tobacco in the world, filling thirty ships a year with millions of pounds of American tobacco and creating a 400 percent trade advantage for America with France.

Making his tobacco trade even more remarkable was his ability to become the largest tobacco supplier in both Britain and France by using trading techniques he invented that kept his identity secret and are now standard in commodities markets.

Although the Asian trade improved Morris revenues, it did little for the rest of America. As revenues tumbled, state assemblies imposed or raised duties on goods imported from other states and imposed or raised property taxes. Farm owners across the country protested, and their states threatened tariff wars. Virginia and Maryland went a step farther, threatening each other with a shooting war over the right to collect duties on ships entering the Potomac River, which separated the two states.

The nation edged to the brink of civil war.

"No treason has operated or can operate so great an injury to America," Robert Morris bellowed in response to the growing interstate feuds. "The payment of debts may indeed be expensive, but it is infinitely more expensive to withhold payment.... The inhabitant of a little hamlet may feel pride in the sense of separate independence. But if there be not one government which can draw forth and direct the combined forces of united America, our independence is but a name, our freedom a shadow, our dignity a dream."[124]

As states vied with each other over tax jurisdictions, farmers protested the rights of state governments to collect taxes. A farmer mutiny erupted in western Massachusetts, where former Captain Daniel Shays, a farmer struggling to keep his property, convinced neighbors that legislators in Boston were colluding with judges and lawyers to raise property taxes and seize farms when farmers found the taxes too high to pay.

With that, he shouted "Close down the courts!" and set off protests that some feared would evolve into a widespread bloody uprising.

Echoing the Shays battle cry, farmers marched to courts across the state and forced them to close and end foreclosures in Massachusetts. Although state militia eventually put down Shays's rebellion, news of his initial success spread elsewhere. In New Hampshire, farmers marched to the state capital at Exeter, surrounded the legislature, and demanded forgiveness of all debts, return of all seized properties to former owners, and equitable distribution of property. A mob of Maryland farmers with similar demands burned down the Charles County courthouse, and Virginia farmers burned down the King William and the New Kent county courthouses.

And back in Massachusetts, Shays followers scored a victory at the polls, voting the governor and three-fourths of the legislature out of office. A new, pro-farmer legislature declared a tax holiday for a year, reduced taxes thereafter, released imprisoned debtor-farmers to go back to work, and exempted clothing, household possessions and tools of trade from seizure in future debt proceedings.

As farmers scored similar victories in neighboring states, the legislators they elected acted to reduce or eliminate duties on trade that crossed state lines.

Along the Potomac River, Maryland and Virginia remained ready to war over claims that their respective borders reached across the river to the opposite shoreline and gave one state or the other exclusive rights to collect fees and duties from passing ships. George Washington, whose Mount Vernon, Virginia, home overlooked the Potomac, stepped into the middle of the dispute.

A private citizen by then, he harvested tons of herring from the Potomac each year. He also owned thousands of acres of undeveloped western land some of which touched Potomac headwaters. He proposed that the two states join in building a network of canals to tie the sources of the Potomac to the headwaters of western rivers.

"Extend the inland navigation of the Eastern waters with those that run...to the Ohio and Lake Erie," Washington enthused, "we shall not only draw the produce of western settlers, but the fur and peltry trade to our ports, to the amazing increase of our exports, while we bind those people to us by a chain that can never be broken."[125]

Bowing to the genius of the father of their country, the two states agreed to end their feud and fund his project together. They agreed to develop and adopt uniform commercial regulations and print a uniform currency–in effect, establishing a commercial union of two states.

But Washington's vision was wider: "We are either a united people or we are not," he asserted. "If the former, let us... act as a nation which has national objects to promote and a national character to support."[126]

Leaders in every state but Rhode Island agreed, and on February 26, 1787, the Confederation Congress resolved that delegates appointed by the assemblies of each state would meet "on the second Monday in May next, at Philadelphia, for the sole and express purpose of revising the Articles of Confederation, and reporting to Congress and to the several Legislatures, such alterations and provisions therein, as shall...render the Federal Constitution adequate to the exigencies of Government and the preservation of the Union."[127]

Although Pennsylvania's Assembly named Benjamin Franklin to its delegation, his advancing age made it necessary for Robert Morris to serve as leader. One of only two delegates who had signed the Declaration of Independence, Morris was conspicuous by his silence. As leader of the host delegation, he opened proceedings, then proposed Washington as Convention president and called for unanimous approval without debate.

After Congress voted "aye" without dissent, Morris ceded the chair to Washington and took his seat with the Philadelphia delegation, but sat through the rest of the convention over the entire summer without stirring or uttering a sound. He excused his behavior saying debate over constitutional provisions was a task for lawyers and that he knew next to nothing about the "science of law."

What he did know, however, was the science of entertaining, of which he was a master. "General Washington," he wrote to his sons Robert Morris III, 18, and Thomas, 16, who were at school in Geneva, Switzerland "is now our guest, having taken up his abode at my house during the time he is to remain in the city.

> There are gentlemen of great abilities employed in this Convention.... You, my children, ought to pray for a successful issue to their labors, as the result is to be a form of

government under which you may hereafter probably have a share, provided you qualify yourselves by a proper application to your studies....[which] are essentially necessary to entitle you to participate in the honor of serving a Free People.[128]

Though stone-faced when chairing the convention, Washington proved a social delight at the Morris mansion. He remained with the Morrises during his entire stay in Philadelphia, playing cards in the evening with Mary Morris, escorting her to a concert, and joining Robert and Mary at Sunday church services. He went romping with Robert, Mary, and the children on weekend outings in the country—fishing and picnicking until dark. The Morrises and Washington would recall their summer weekends together as some of the happiest moments in their collective lives.

Although he remained all-but-silent on the convention floor, Morris used his entertaining skills in the comfort of his living and dining rooms to instruct delegates in the advantages of free enterprise.

Morris charged that interprovincial duties in other countries raised prices artificially, produced shortages and, often, widespread famine and rioting. Without such restrictions, he argued, American craftsmen and manufacturers large and small would be able to draw from endless supplies of duty-free American raw materials—timber, iron, coal, minerals of all kinds.

Intra-coastal waters and good roads would offer safe transport and give American manufacturers enormous advantages over British competitors who depended on imports and risk-fraught transoceanic transport. Absent state-imposed duties on southern cotton, for example, New England's weavers and textile producers would be able to buy cotton at prices low enough to compete with British textile manufacturers and eventually become the world's largest textile industry.

Virginia's James Madison agreed, describing New Jersey as a patient bleeding from both arms. Without a port of its own, it was forced to import foreign goods and export its own goods through ports in New York and Pennsylvania, each of which charged import and export duties on all goods going in and out of New Jersey.

In the end Morris's cajoling convinced delegates to write and sign a document that transferred control of interstate commerce from the states to the federal government and converted the Morris dream of a "common market" into reality. The Constitution and its interstate commerce clause would eventually transform the United States into the most prosperous and productive nation on earth, allowing goods and services to cross all state borders duty-free.

On September 17, 1787, after four months of debate, delegates from twelve states (Rhode Island had refused to participate) completed their work writing the Constitution. Robert Morris and 38 others thereupon signed the document, which Morris called "a work from Heaven.

"Others have given it a less righteous origin," he opined. "I have many reasons to believe it is the work of plain, honest men....Faulty it must be, for what is perfect? But if adopted, experience will, I believe, show that its faults are just the reverse of what they are supposed to be."[129]

For Morris, his signature was his third on each of the nation's founding documents—the Declaration of Independence, the Articles of Confederation, and the Constitution. Although a few more honors awaited, it would be the highlight of his political life and mark the beginning of what would be a precipitous fall from the summit of American political, financial, and social life.

On September 30, 1788, however, Morris won election as one of Pennsylvania's first two United States Senators. Taking his seat, he eagerly joined in the constitutionally assigned tasks of establishing a federal judiciary and various departments in the executive branch. On

April 9, 1789, the Electoral College voted unanimously to seat George Washington as the nation's first President.

On April 14, George Washington received official notification of his election as the nation's first president and set out from Mount Vernon on a triumphal two-week journey to New York, where he would take the oath of office on April 30.

Robert Morris welcomed the president-elect en route, but to avoid any public display of favoritism, Washington declined the Morris invitation to stay at the Morris home and spent the night at the City Tavern.

It was in Philadelphia, however, that Washington quietly offered Morris the post of Secretary of the Treasury in the new administration, and, to the president-elect's surprise, Morris turned it down, saying a move to New York would create too many family and business problems.

In fact, Morris had suffered serious financial reversals after one of his major suppliers filed for bankruptcy and failed to deliver £20,000 of tobacco that Morris had not only presold but had pledged to reinvest the expected proceeds.

As creditors demanded that Morris make good on his pledge, he found himself denied the credit he need to pursue his business. He was hardly in a position to accept a post as United States Secretary of the Treasury.

Never at a loss for novel business schemes, however, Morris enlisted trusted intermediaries to buy and sell on his behalf (for handsome commissions, of course). Coupled with investments in western lands, the new trading arrangements eventually restored Morris business revenues and profits—but only barely.

In the meantime, Washington—at Morris's recommendation—named Alexander Hamilton Secretary of Treasury. Hamilton had been Washington's aide during the war and his ties by marriage to the banking industry made him a logical choice.

In mid-May, Martha Washington set out with her two grandchildren to join her husband in New York. Unlike her husband, she had no qualms about staying at the Morris home in Philadelphia with her friend Mary Morris. After three days Mary Morris and her eight-year-old daughter Maria accompanied Martha and the two Washington grand-children to New York to join their husbands.

To their astonishment and joy, Washington and Morris awaited to greet their ladies at the Hudson River landing in New Jersey and escort them on a magnificently decorated barge across the water to New York and the cheers of the huge festive crowd that awaited.

With the new government in place, Robert Morris returned to the Senate to press for passage of his three pet monetary reforms, which the Confederation Congress had rejected: funding the debt, creation of a mint, and decimalization of the currency. Morris faced fervent opposition, however, from southern senators, whose states had spent little during the war and refused to help pay a penny of the heavy war debts incurred by northern states.

At the urging of Alexander Hamilton, Virginia Representative James Madison, and the newly appointed Secretary of State Thomas Jefferson, convinced enough southern opponents of funding to switch votes in exchange for northern support for situating the proposed federal capital city in Virginia.

In April 1792, Congress passed the other great Morris monetary reforms: the Mint Act, which created the U.S. mint and decimalized U.S. currency.

With fulfillment of his most fervent legislative ambitions, Morris's interest in politics waned and allowed him to turn his attention to his first loves: his family and his business. Ironically, it was an unexpected action by the impotent Confederation Congress that reignited his lifelong fervor for making money.

In its last days of existence, the Confederation Congress passed the Northwest Ordinance, by which Virginia and other states startled

Americans by ceding their unsettled western lands to the federal government.

Comprising modern-day Ohio, Indiana, Illinois, Michigan, Wisconsin, and Minnesota, the Northwest Territory became a target of intense speculation for western European immigrants flocking to the New World in search of individual liberties and economic opportunities denied them by Europe's nobility and absolute monarchs. In addition, thousands of Americans in the East, many of them younger sons blocked from inheriting family farms by rules of primogeniture, flocked west to claim lands. of their own.

Robert Morris and members of America's wealthy political class anticipated the demand and bought millions of acres of virgin wilderness in the West at prices Congress had set low enough to ensure a flow of revenues to help clear war-time debts.

Morris snapped up one million acres and sold them within three years at three times his purchase price. His success sparked a national frenzy, with former Major General Henry Knox, Arthur Lee, Robert Livingston and even President Washington investing all the cash they could gather or borrow to buy land.

All of them embraced a Morris vision of millions fleeing British and European economic tyranny and flocking westward across America, clearing forests, planting fields, building homes, constructing roads, canals, and railways, and forming vast numbers of new businesses and industries. For the first time in history, commoners would own land instead of leasing it from noblemen—and keep the proceeds of their labor for themselves.

In 1790, Congress passed—and Washington signed—the Residence Act of 1790, by which Congress would acquire vacant land along the Potomac River to become the seat of the national government in 1800. In the meantime, the government would remain in New York until 1792, at which time it would move to Philadelphia until 1800. Although Philadelphia remained America's largest, most prosperous city, finding a residence and office space for Washington's huge household and political enterprise presented a challenge—until Robert Morris offered the President his and Mary's house—by then the most lavish residence in Philadelphia.

The offer proved beneficial for both the Washington and Morris families after the Morrises were able to buy and move into a house close to the President's house. The two families—especially Mary and Martha—would mingle almost daily and embark together on family excursions into the nearby countryside on weekends.

With each foray into the country, Morris grew ever more enthused about the opportunities to develop wilderness lands into prosperous farms.

Indeed, he grew so enthusiastic that he violated his normally conservative trading principles by mingling borrowed funds with his capital and investing both in undeveloped land. In doing so, he converted productive financial reserves into unproductive non-convertible assets.

At one point, he added four million acres in western Pennsylvania, investing almost $700,000 of his own funds and borrowing $100,000 more to take advantage of a drop from 80 to 20 cents an acre.

As Morris continued his relentless spending, his friend the President grew concerned, imploring Morris to end his buying spree and reduce the enormous debt he was accumulating.

"My dear General," Morris replied to Washington, "I can never do things in the small. I must either be a man or a mouse."[130]

Refusing to be a mouse and convinced he would soon be able to convert his holdings into millions, Morris commissioned French architect Pierre L'Enfant to build a new mansion in Philadelphia for Mary. Congress had engaged L'Enfant to design the new federal capital city, and Morris commissioned him to build Mary "the grandest [house] ever attempted in America."

As wide and deep as two houses, two stories high, clad in marble, filled with the finest English furniture, it was to rank in grandeur with London's Buckingham Palace.

French crystal chandeliers and sconces would light its interiors; Dutch oil paintings and Flemish tapestries would line its walls; Greek and Roman sculptures would greet passers-by in every hallway; guests would dine off rare Chinese and French porcelain services and feed themselves with the finest French and English sterling silver....

As crates of Morris purchases piled up on Philadelphia docks, even his architect marveled at what all Philadelphia now called "Morris's folly."

Robert Morris's "Folly."

Then, in mid-August, all work at the Morris mansion suddenly stopped!

Yellow fever had struck Philadelphia in epidemic proportions. All who could afford to do so fled the city. More than one-third of the city's 55,000 people left, and by the time a mid-October frost ended the plague, more than 5,000 of those who had stayed in town—ten percent of the city's population—had perished.

Adding to America's turmoil, France and England went to war—on land and sea. President Washington incurred the wrath of both nations by declaring the United States neutral. Both nations retaliated, sinking more than 500 American ships and paralyzing American foreign trade. Atlantic ocean traffic halted, ending the flow of European immigrants to America. European banks stopped lending to buyers of American land, ending the flow of foreign funds to the United States. Land values in the West plunged!

Initially, Morris misjudged the drop in land values as a buying opportunity, and, like a man possessed, he plunged deeper in debt, extending his credit to the limit, borrowing to buy land at what he was certain were bargain prices. He bought 30,000 more acres in Ohio, 44,000 more in Virginia....

Mary begged him to stop. Washington begged him to stop. He responded by buying 250 liters of the best Bordeaux wines he could find to celebrate what he was certain would be his greatest financial miracle.

Before the wines arrived, however, a parade of debt collectors marched to his door in Philadelphia demanding full payment for all his purchases and investments. Some of America's most distinguished political leaders had also bought land on credit, and, like Morris, lacked cash to cover their debts. Sheriffs arrested them all and marched them off to debtor's prison. Among the most distinguished debtors: U.S. Supreme Court Associate Justice James Wilson, a signer with Morris of both the Declaration of Independence and the Constitution and owner of the "Fort Wilson" mansion.

"I am seriously uneasy," Morris finally admitted. "Mr. Wilson's affair will make the vultures more keen after me."

Morris retreated to "The Hills," which he renamed "Castle Defiance" after turning away squads of debt collectors. He fired a barrage of letters to his most influential United States and European contacts, promising enormous returns if they would lend him cash or extend him additional credit. Most letters went unanswered, and none produced a penny's worth of relief.

Just before the new year in 1797, a sheriff and six deputies marched up to The Hills with axes and sledge hammers and began to break down the mansion door. Morris and a few friends were armed and ready, and, as he had done at "Fort Wilson," the great capitalist fired and forced the would-be invaders to retreat.

"They would have had me in five minutes if every pistol and gun had not been manned and fixed at them," Morris boasted.

In the weeks that followed, however, his creditors replaced bullets with a barrage of court orders that separated Morris from all his assets—200,000 acres of North Carolina lands; homes and half-built homes in Washington; even a chariot—"one of the best that was ever built in America," according to the sheriff.

"No man can be more strongly impressed than I am with the cruelty of our situation, which exposes us to the loss of an immense fortune merely from the caprice and whims of overcautious individuals who think there is no safety in the value of lots or lands," he lamented to accountant John Nicholson, a recent trading partner.

"I have no money nor any prospect of receiving it.... I cannot borrow for nobody will lend. I cannot sell anything that will command money."

Later, he added, "As events have turned up, it becomes a duty to submit to fate, to meet the bad as well as the good with fortitude, and to make the best of whatever happens. My health is good, my spirits not broke, my mind sound and vigorous, and therefore I will do all I can consistently with principles of integrity to make the best of my affairs and extricate myself as well as I can."

Out of funds, indeed out of bullets to ward off the sheriff and his deputies, Morris finally surrendered to the inevitable, admitting in his diary, "My money is gone, my furniture is to be sold, and I am to go to prison and my family to starve. Good night."

As Mary Morris cried hysterically, the sheriff led her husband to Philadelphia's debtor's prison, only two blocks from the Morris family townhouse and a block from the Pennsylvania State House where he had signed the nation's three founding documents.

Philadelphia's Walnut Street Prison.

Although many Founding Fathers had lost fortunes following investment advice from Robert Morris, none gloated over his fall; indeed, most stood by him, visiting him regularly and ensuring Mary's comforts in modest quarters they rented for her by the prison. They even bribed prison guards to secure "private quarters" for Morris. He called his prison a "hotel with grated doors" in letters he wrote to friends, inviting them to dine.

In 1798, retired President George Washington walked to debtor's prison to visit his old friend and dine with him and Mary in Robert's cell for what would be their last moments together.

Mary sat and listened to the quiet intercourse of the two devoted friends—the one, the founder of America's military and political system; the other, the founder of its economic system. Together, they were the voices of America's past, speaking of a future neither would live to see. Washington died a year later, on December 14, 1799.

Three months before his death, however, Washington learned that Mary Morris had lost her former mansion.

"We hope it is unnecessary to repeat," he wrote from his home at Mount Vernon,, "how happy we would be to see you and [20-year-old daughter Maria] Miss Morris under our roof and for as long a stay as you find convenient...for be assured we ever have, and still do retain, the most affectionate regard for you, Mr. Morris, and the family."

Mary paid the steepest personal price for Morris's financial misadventures. Once one of Philadelphia's wealthiest heiresses and most gracious hostesses, she spent the years of her husband's imprisonment mired in near-poverty.

"She endeavored to smile away the melancholy," Abigail Adams said of Mary Morris after visiting her and her husband in debtor's prison. "I requested her to come and take tea with me! I took her by the hand. She said she did not visit but would not refuse the pleasure of coming someday when I was alone. She then turned from me, and the tears burst forth."

Ironically, Abigail and her husband President John Adams were living in the mansion Robert Morris had once owned and where Mary Morris had spent her happiest years as Philadelphia's reigning queen of Philadelphia society.

Morris emerged from prison on August 26, 1801, and in early December, a bankruptcy commission found it useless to continue further proceedings against him. By then, the bankruptcy court had sold all his assets and personal possessions and extracted his last penny.

Ever the optimist, Morris strutted out of prison, his head held high! And with good reason. He had owned more land, more ships, and more personal property and commanded more wealth than any man in America and had paid the troops of the Continental Army from his own pocket to fight a seven-year war with the world's most powerful nation. After Washington himself, Robert Morris had done more than anyone to win America's War of Independence. He had no reason to believe he could not rebuild his life and his fortune.

"I now find myself a free citizen of the United States without one cent that I can call my own," he wrote to his son Thomas. "I am on the lookout for something to do that will give me bread. I will not be idle."[131]

With that, he rode to Washington City, as it was called then, to visit the new President, Thomas Jefferson, and his Secretary of State James Madison. Both received him warmly. Jefferson even considered appointing Morris Secretary of Treasury before deciding the appointment would provoke too much controversy.

Within a year of Morris's release from prison, a group of merchants sent his hopes for the future soaring with an offer to become president of a new bank. But it failed the day before it was to open and ended his last business opportunity. Robert Morris had run out of financial miracles.

He died on May 8, 1708 at the age of 71 and was buried in Philadelphia's Christ Church cemetery near his friends, Founding Fathers Benjamin Franklin and U.S. Supreme Court Justice James Wilson. He left his surviving family next to nothing—only a few token gifts such as a gold watch, a gold-headed cane that John Hancock had given him, and so forth. Mary survived him by twenty-one years. Of his children, only one—Thomas, the second oldest—went into public service as a lawyer and a congressman.

Having fathered capitalism and the free enterprise system in America, Robert Morris empowered millions to stream across America's vast wilderness, free of federal rules, regulations, and taxes in what became the world's first common market.

With every state in the union accessible by all, without encumbrances, Americans carved farms, villages, towns, and cities out of the wilds; built roads, canals and railways to unite the states economically, factories and businesses that enriched the American people, and buildings taller than any the world had ever seen. The system of free enterprise that Morris fathered allowed the United States to stage an economic and industrial revolution that transformed America into the economic wonder of the industrialized world.

Bibliography

Thomas Perkins Abernathy, *Western Lands and the American Revolution* (New York: D. Appleton-Century Company, 1937).

Adams Family Correspondence (Cambridge, MA: Belknap Press of Harvard University Press, 10 vols., L.H. Butterfield, ed.)

Diana E. Ascott, *Liverpool 1660 to 1750* (Liverpool: Liverpool University Press, 2011).

Thomas Willing Balch, *Willing Letters and Papers, Edited with a Biographical Essay of Thomas Willing of Philadelphia (1731-1821),* (Philadelphia: Allen, Lane and Scott, 1922).

George Bancroft, *History of the United States, from the Discovery of the American Continent* (Boston: Little, Brown and Company, 10 vols.., 1866).

William Russell Birch, *Life of Robert Morris, the Great Financier* (Philadelphia: Desilver Publisher, 1841).

Patricia Brady, *Martha Washington, An American Life* (New York: Viking Penguin Group, 2005).

Helen Bryan, *Martha Washington, First Lady of Liberty* (New York: John Wiley & Sons, 2002).

Congress: *Journals of the Continental Congress, 1774-1789* (Washington, D.C.: Government Printing Office, Worthington Chauncey Ford, ed., 1904)

" *Letters of Delegates to Congress, 1774-1789* (Washington, DC: Library of Congress, 1979, 26 vols., Edward C. Burnett; Paul H. Smith, eds., 1979)

" *Letters of the Members of the Continental Congress* (Washington, D.C., 1921-1936, 7 vols., Edmund C. Burnett, ed.)

" *Papers of the Continental Congress, 1774-1789,* National Archives, Washington, D.C.

Silas Deane, *The Deane Papers, 1782-1790* (New York: The New York Historical Society, 1891, 23 vols.).

Daniel Defoe, *A Tour Thro' the Whole Island of Great Britain* (London: J.M. Dent and Co., 1927).

John Dickinson, *The Writings of John Dickinson* (Philadelphia: The Historical Society of Pennsylvania, 2 vols.,1895)

Thomas M. Doerflinger, *A Vigorous Spirit of Enterprise: Merchants and Economic Development in Revolutionary Philadelphia* (New York: The

University of North Carolina Press, 1986).

Henri Doniol, *Histoire de la Participation de la France à l'Établissement des États-Unis d'Amérique* (Paris: Imprimerie Nationale, 1886, 5 vols., quarto)

Elizabeth Drinker, The Diary of Elizabeth Drinker (Boston: Northeastern University Press Elaine Forman Crane, ed., 3 vols., 1991).

Dr. William Duncan, *Report on the Sanitary Condition of Liverpool* (London: W. Clowes and Sons, 1839).

Peter Earle, *Sailors: English Merchant Seamen*, 1650-1775 (London: Methuen, 2007)

E. James Ferguson, *The Power of the Purse: A History of American Public Finance, 1776-1990* (Chapel Hill: University of North Carolina Press, 1961).

Henry Fielding, *The Journal of a Voyage to Lisbon* (London: A. Millar, 1755)

John C. Fitzpatrick, ed., *The Writings of George Washington, from the Original Manuscript Sources, 1745-1799* (Washington: United States Government Printing Office, 1931-44, 39 vols.).

Peter Force, *American Archives*, (Washington, D.C., 1837-1853).

Benjamin Franklin, *The Works of Benjamin Franklin* (New York: G. P. Putnam's Sons, 1904, 12 vols.).

Douglas Southall Freeman, *George Washington* (New York: Charles Scribner's Sons, 1951, 7 vols.).

Henry Lawrence Gipson, *The Coming of the Revolution, 1763-1775* (New York: Harper & Brothers, 1954).

Alan Greenspan, Adrian Wooldridge, *Capitalism in America: A History* (New York: Penguin Press, 2018).

John Steele Gordon, *An Empire of Wealth: The Epic History of American Economic Power* (New York: HarperCollins Publishers, 2004).

Alexander Hamilton, *The Papers of Alexander Hamilton* (New York: Columbia University Press, 1961-1987, 27 vols.).

Alexander Hamilton, James Madison, John Jay, *The Federalist* (New York: J. and A. McLean, 1787).

John Hancock, *John Hancock His Book* (Boston: Lee and Shepard; A. E. Brown, ed., 1898).

William Wirt Henry, *Patrick Henry: Life, Correspondence and Speeches* (New York: Charles Scribner's Sons, 1891, 3 vols.)

John Jay, *The Correspondence and Public Papers of John Jay, 1763-1826* (New York: G.P. Putnam's Sons, 4 vols., 1890-1893).

Journals of the Continental Congress, 1774-1789 (Washington: U.S. Government Printing Office, 1904-1937, 34 vols.)

Joseph J. Kelley, Jr., *Life and Times in Colonial Philadelphia* (Harrisburg, PE: The Stackpole Company, 1973).

Richard Henry Lee, *The Life of Arthur Lee, LL.D.* (Boston: Wells and Lilly, 2 vols., 1829).

Richard H. Lee, *Memoir of the Life of Richard Henry Lee and His Correspondence* (Philadelphia: H. C. Carey and I. Lea, 1825, 2 vols.).

William Lee, *Letters of William Lee, 1766-1783* (Brooklyn, NY, Historical Printing Club, 1891, 3 vols., Worthington Chauncey Ford, ed.).

Richard Henry Lee, *The Life of Arthur Lee, LL.D.* (Boston: Wells and Lilly, 1829, 2 vols.).

Letters of Delegates to Congress, 1774-1789 (Washington, D.C.: Library of Congress, 25 vols., Paul H. Smith et al, eds. 1976-2000).

Life in Early Philadelphia: Documents from the Revolutionary and Early National Periods (University Parks, PE: The Pennsylvania State University Press, 1995, Billy G. Smith, ed.).

Louis de Loménie, *Beaumarchais et son temps: Études sur la société en France au XVIIIe siècle*

Liverpool University Press, 2011).

Eric Martone, *Encyclopedia of Blacks in European History and Culture* (Westport, CT: Greenwood Press, 2009, 2 vols.).

Herman Melville, *Redburn* (Hammondsworth: Penguin, 1986 [1849]), 192.

Gouverneur Morris, *Gouverneur Morris Papers, 1768-1816* (Columbia University Rare Book and Manuscript Library, New York, NY)).

Robert Morris, *Account of Robert Morris' Property* (Philadelphia: Stan V. Henkels, Auction Commission Merchant, 1917).

" *The Confidential Correspondence of Robert Morris* (Philadelphia: The University of Pittsburgh Press, 1975, 9 vols.).

" *The Papers of Robert Morris, 1781-1784* (Pittsburgh: The University of Pittsburgh Press, 1975, 9 vols.).

Ellis Paxson Oberholtzer, *Robert Morris: Patriot and Financier* (New York: The Macmillan Company, 1903).

Elizabeth Powel, Manuscripts, Washington Library, Mount Vernon, VA.

Samuel Powel, Powel Family Papers, The Historical Society of Pennsylvania, Philadelphia, PA.

Charles Rappleye, *Robert Morris, Financier of the American Revolution* (New York: Simon & Schuster, 2010).

William B. Reed, *The Life and Correspondence of Joseph Reed* (Philadelphia: Lindsay and Blakiston, 1847, 2 vols.)

David Richardson, *Liverpool and the English Slave Trade* (Liverpool: Liverpool University Press, 2010).

Arthur M. Schlesinger, *The Colonial Merchants and the American Revolution* (New York: Athenium, 1968).

Harlow Giles Unger, *John Hancock: Merchant King and American Patriot* (New York: John Wiley & Sons, 2000).

" *Thomas Paine and the Clarion Call for American Independence* (Boston: Da Capo Press, 2019).

Clarence Ver Steeg, *Robert Morris, Revolutionary Financier* (Philadelphia: University of Pennsylvania Press, 1954),

George Washington, *The Diaries of George Washington* (Charlottesville: University Press of Virginia, 6 vols., Donald Jackson and Dorothy Twohig, eds., 1976-1979), 1:195.

" *The Papers of George Washington, Colonial Series, 1748-August 1755* (Charlottesville: University Press of Virginia, 1983-1995, 10 vols.).

" *The Papers of George Washington, Confederation Series* (Charlottesville: The University of Virginia Press, 6 vols.,, 1992-1997).

" *The Papers of George Washington, Presidential Series* (Charlottesville: The University of Virginia Press, multiple volumes, 1987-in progress).

" *The Papers of George Washington, Revolutionary Series* (Charlottesville, VA: University Press of Virginia, multiple volumes, 1997- in progress).

" *The Papers of George Washington, Retirement Series* (Charlottesville, Virginia: University Press of Virginia, 1998-1999, 4 vols., W.W. Abbott, ed.)

" *The Writings of George Washington, from the Original Manuscript Sources 1745-1799* (Washington, D.C.: U.S. Government Printing Office, John C. Fitzpatrick, ed., 39 vols., 1931-1944).

Anne Hollingsworth Wharton, *Salons Colonial and Republican* (Philadelphia: J.B. Lippincott Company, 1900).

Collections

The Deane Papers, (New York: Collections of the New York Historical Society for the year 1888, 1889, 5 vols.).

Periodicals
  Graham's Magazine
  Pennsylvania Chronicle
  Pennsylvania Journal and Weekly Advertiser
  The Pennsylvania Magazine of History and Biography
  Pennsylvania Packet
  Virginia Gazette
  William & Mary Quarterly

[1] Daniel Defoe, *A Tour Thro' the Whole Island of Great Britain* (London: J.M. Dent and Co., 1927). [Originally published in parts from 1724 to 1727.]

[2] David Richardson, *Liverpool and the English indentured Trade* (Liverpool: Liverpool University Press, 2010).

[3] In August 2000, the Liverpool City Council issued a formal apology for the town's role in the 18th-century slave trade.

[4] Ibid.,

[5] Herman Melville, *Redburn* (Hammondsworth: Penguin, 1986 [1849]), 192.

[6] Henry Fielding, *The Journal of a Voyage to Lisbon* (London: A. Millar, 1755), 68.

[7] Daniel Defoe, cited in Peter Earle, *Sailors: English Merchant Seamen, 1650-1775* (London: Methuen, 2007)

[8] Dr. William Duncan, *Report on the Sanitary Condition of Liverpool* (London: W. Clowes and Sons, 1839).

[9] In an era before the discovery of crop rotation to reinvigorate the land, Maryland's tobacco crops extracted so much of the nutrients in the soil that commercial tobacco production in the state ended by the turn of the next century.

[10] *Pennsylvania Journal and Weekly Advertiser,* May 6, 1762, No. 1013, cited in Thomas Willing Balch, *Willing Letters and Papers* (Philadelphia: Allen, Lane and Scott, 1922), 20-21.

[11] The City Council appointed him mayor of Philadelphia in 1763 and the Pennsylvania Supreme Court in 1767—the last such appointment under British rule.

[12] George Washington, *The Diaries of George Washington* (Charlottesville: University Press of Virginia, 6 vols., Donald Jackson and Dorothy Twohig, eds., 1976-1979), 1:195.

[13] A term derived from the Spanish *sobre + cargo.*

[14] T. Willing to RM, April 27, 1778, Thomas Willing Balch, *Willing Letters and Papers* (Philadelphia: Allen, Lane and Scott, 1922), 85.

[15] *Pennsylvania Journal,* September 29, 1763, p. 5., in Balch, 22.

[16] Ibid., April 18, 1765, in Balch, 27.

[17] A cask holding about 63 gallons.

[18] William Russell Birch, *Life of Robert Morris, the Great Financier* (Philadelphia: Desilver Publisher, 1841), 4.

[19] RM to William Hooper, January 18, 1777, in Clarence Ver Steeg, *Robert Morris, Revolutionary Financier* (Philadelphia: University of Pennsylvania Press, 1954), citing Morris *MSS*, Misc., Historical Society of Pennsylvania.

[20] John Hancock, *John Hancock His Book* (Boston: Lee and Shepard; A. E. Brown, ed.,
1898), 61-64.

[21] John Hancock to Jonathan Bernard, October 14, 1765, in Harlow Giles Unger, *John Hancock: Merchant King and American Patriot* (New York: John Wiley & Sons, 2000), 98.

[22] Ibid., 92.

[23] Declaration of the Stamp Act Congress, October 1765, cited in Henry Lawrence Gipson, *The Coming of the Revolution, 1763-1775* (New York: Harper & Brothers, 1954), 100.

[24] George Washington to Francis Dandridge, September 20, 1765, W. W. Abbott and Dorothy Twohig, eds., *The Papers of George Washington, Colonial Series, 1748-August 1755* (Charlottesville: University Press of Virginia, 1983-1995, 10 vols.), 7:395-396.

[25] A term Willing frequently used in writing to Morris, cited here from Thomas Willing to Robert Morris, April 27, 1788, Balch, 76-85.

[26] Unger, *John Hancock,* 106.

[27] John Hancock to William Reeve, September 3, 1767, in Unger, *John Hancock,* 113.

[28] PGW Colonial, 10:128-31, George Washington to Bryan Fairfax, July 20, 1774.

[29] For complete text of Dickinson's Letters, see Leicester Ford, ed., *The Writings of John Dickinson* (1895), 307-406

[30] RM to (?), December 9, 1775, *LDC*, 2:471.

[31] RM to James Duff, February 26, 1775, Morris Papers, New York Public Library.

[4]

[32] Joseph Shippen, *Lines Written in an Assembly Room* (Philadelphia: Crissy and Markley, Thomas Balch, ed., 1855), LXXII-LXXIV.

[33] An Address by Charles Henry Hart, June 7, 1877, published in *The Pennsylvania Magazine of History and Biography,* Vol. 2, No. 2, (1878), pp. 157-184.

[34] Mary White Morris to Esther White, April 14, 1777, quoted in address by Charles Henry Hart, ibid.

[35] Anne Hollingsworth Wharton, *Salons Colonial and Republican* (Philadelphia: J.B. Lippincott Company, 1908), 131.

[36] RM, to Benjamin Harrison, December 29, 1776, *Letters of Delegates to Congress, 1774-1789* (Washington, DC: Library of Congress, 1979, 26 vols., Edward C. Burnett; Paul H. Smith, eds., 1979), 5:693-694. [Hereafter, *LDC.*]

[37] Wharton, *Salons...*", citing Major General François Jean de Beauvoir Marquis de Chastellux, 131.

[38] RM to Joseph Reed, July 21, 1776, *LDC*, 2:19.

[39] Rules and Regulations of the Continental Association, *Journals of the Continental Congress, 1774-1789* (Washington, D.C.: Worthington Chauncey Ford, ed., 1904), 1:75-80.

[40] RM to James Duff, February 26, 1775, Morris Papers, New York Public Library.

[41] William Wirt Henry, *Patrick Henry: Life, Correspondence and Speeches* (New York: Charles Scribner's Sons, 1891, 3 vols.) 3:266.

[42] Armed civilian boys and men who volunteered to be ready to fight the British at a "minute's" notice.

[44] Doniol, *Histoire de la participation de la France,* 1:267; 287-292.

[45] RM to Unknown, December 9, 1775, *LDC*, 2:471.

[46] Ibid.

[47] RM to William Hooper, January 18, 1777, in Clarence Ver Steeg, *Robert Morris, Revolutionary Financier* (Philadelphia: University of Pennsylvania Press, 1954), citing Morris *MSS*, Misc., Historical Society of Pennsylvania.

[48] RM to Joseph Reed, July 21, 1776, *LDC*, 2:18-20.

[49] Richard Henry Lee, The Virginia Resolution for Independence, June 7, 1776, *Papers of the Continental Congress, 1774-1789*, National Archives, Washington, D.C.

[50] John Adams to Abigail Adams, July 3, 1776, in *Adams Family Correspondence* (Cambridge, MA: Belknap Press of Harvard University Press, 10 vols., L.H. Butterfield, ed.), 2:29-33.

[2] Douglas Southall Freeman, *George Washington* (New York: Charles Scribner's Sons, 1951, 7 vols.),

IV:194n.

[52] RM to Joseph Reed [Pennsylvania president], July 20, 1776 , Peter Force, *American Archives*, Series V, 3 vols., I:467.

[53] RM, *The Papers of Robert Morris* [henceforth, *RM Papers*] (Pittsburgh, PA, University of Pittsburgh Press, E James Ferguson, ed., 9 vols., 1973), 1:399.

[54] Merchant-bankers were tradesmen peculiar to America's barter system. Without hard money to buy tools, for example, a farmer would pledge part of his future crop to the merchant, who, in turn, "loaned" tools to the farmer, much as a banker lends money today. Repaid with a portion of the farmer's crops, the farmer kept his tools while the merchant-banker resold the crops he received for other goods or, if possible, for cash. Either way, he functioned as both merchant and banker, hence the term that was common in 18th century America.

[55] Robert Morris to Silas Deane, August 11, 1776, "The Deane Papers," Collections of the New York Historical Society for the year 1886 (New York, 1887), v. 19, p.174.

[56] RM to John Ross, August 11, 1776, *LDC*.

[57] RM to Silas Deane, August 11, 1776, *LDC*.

[58] John Hancock, in Congress, October 1, 1776 , Peter Force, *American Archives* (Washington, D.C.: 1837-53, Series V, 3 vols..) II:823.

[59] RM to John Bradford, October 8, 1776, *LDC*.

[60] John Hancock to RM, January 14, 1777, *Letters of the Members of the Continental Congress* (Washington, D.C., 1921-1936, 7 vols., Edmund C. Burnett, ed.), 2:215.

[61] RM to George Washington, , December 23, 1776, Peter Force, *American Archives*, 1330.

[62] George Washington to John Augustine Washington, November 16-19, 1776, PGWR, 7:102-105.

[63] George Washington to Lund Washington, December 10-17, 1776, *The Papers of George Washington, Revolutionary War Series* (Charlottesville: University Press of Virginia, multi-volume in progress),7:289-292.

[64] George Bancroft, *History of the United States, from the Discovery of the American Continent* (Boston: Little, Brown and Company, 10 vols.., 1866), III: 241.

[65] RM to George Washington, January 1, 1777, *LDC*

[66] RM to George Washington, February 27, 1777, *LDC.*

[67] George Washington to RM, March 2, 1777, *LDC.*

[68] John Ross to Silas Deane, July 30, 1777, *Deane Papers*, II:77; 155.

[69] *Willing Letters,* 41

[70] RM to Richard Peters, January 25, 1778, *LDC.*

[71] RM to Committee of Commerce, December 17, 1777, *LDC. **RM TO BROTHER***

[72] RM to Henry Laurens, December 26, 1777.

[73] Elizabeth Drinker, he Diary of Elizabeth Drinker (Boston: Northeastern University Press Elaine Forman Crane, ed., 3 vols., 1991), I:306.

[74] George Washington to John Augustine Washington, July 4, 1778, PGWR, 16:25-26.

[75] Richard Henry Lee, *The Life of Arthur Lee, LL.D.* (Boston: Wells and Lilly, 1829, 2 vols.), 2:124, 127-128.

[76] Thomas Paine, "The Affair of Silas Deane," in the *Pennsylvania Packet,* December 15, 1778; "To the Public on Mr. Deane's Affair, *Pennsylvania Packet,* December 31, 1778, *TP Writings*, 1:395-408; 409-437. See also Harlow Giles Unger, *Thomas Paine and the Clarion Call for American Independence* (Boston: Da Capo Press, 2019), 89.

3 Benjamin Franklin to RM (undated), The Works of Benjamin Franklin, (New York: G.P. Putnam's Sons, 1904, 12 vols., IX, 14).

1 Thomas Paine, "The Affair of Silas Deane," in the *Pennsylvania Packet*, December 15, 1778; "To the Public on Mr. Deane's Affair, *Pennsylvania Packet*, December 31, 1778, *TP Writings*, 1:395-408; 409-437.

[2] Statement of Robert Morris "To the Public," *The Deane Papers* (New York: Collections of the New York Historical Society for the year 1888, 1889, 5 vols.) 3:260-266. See also Charles Rappleye, *Robert Morris, Financier of the American Revolution* (New York: Simon & Schuster, 2010), 170-171.

1 George Washington to Benjamin Harrison, December 18, 1778, PGWR, 18:447-452.

[81] John Alexander, "The Fort Wilson Incident of 1779: A Study of the Revolutionary Crowd," *William & Mary Quarterly*, 3rd Series) V. 31, p.589.

[82] *Pennsylvania Packet*, July 15, 1779.

[83] C. Page Smith, "The Attack on Fort Wilson," (*Pennsylvania Magazine of History and Biography*, Vol. 78,, No. 2, p. 177-188), 187.

[84] Henry Laurens to John Adams, October 4, 1779, *LDC*.

[85] Thomas Perkins Abernathy, *Western Lands and the American Revolution* (New York: D. Appleton-Century Company, 1937), 173.

[86] George Washington to Joseph Reed, December 16, 1779, *The Life and Correspondence of Joseph Reed* (Philadelphia: Lindsay and Blakiston, 1847, 2 vols.), II:190.

[87] RM to Stacey Hepburn, December 12, 1779, *RM Papers*, Queens College, New York.

[88] Redwood Fisher, "Revolutionary Reminiscences Connected with the Life of Robert Morris," *Graham's Magazine*, v. 44, p. 19, in Rappeleye, 211.,

[89] George Washington to Joseph Reed, May 28, 1780, *The Writings of George Washington*, 18:434-440.

[90] Ibid.

[91] RM, *Robert Morris Papers,* 1:399

[92] RM to the President of Congress, July 17, 1781, 1:397-402.

[93] George Washington to [Pennsylvania President] Joseph Reed, May 28, 1780, *The Writings of George Washington*, 18:434-440.

[94] Although the title remained the same, the former post of Superintendent of Finance was responsible to Congress alone—not to the nation of the United States formed under the Articles of Confederation..

[95] RM Diary, February 21, 1781, in *RM Papers*, 1:8-9.

[96] Alexander Hamilton to Robert Morris, April 30, 1781, ibid., 1:31-60.

[97] Benjamin Franklin to RM, July 26, 1781, ibid., 1:391.

[98] John Swanwick to Robert Morris, February 20, 1781, ibid., 1:5-8.

[99] George Washington to Lund Washington, December 10-17th, 1776, *The Papers of George Washington, Revolutionary Series* (Charlottesville, VA: University Press of Virginia, multiple volumes, 1997- in progress), 7:289-292.

[100] RM To the President of Congress, March 13, 1781, *RM Papers*, 1:17-19.

[101] Ibid., May 14, 1781, 1:62-64.

[102] Benjamin Franklin to RM, July 26, 1781, ibid., 1:391.

[103] George Washington to RM, June 4, 1781, *The Writings of George Washington*, 22:159

[104] RM Diary, May 28, 1781, *RM Papers,* 1:82.

[105] RM to Thomas Lowrey, May 29, 1781, ibid, 1:90-91..,

[106] RM to Philip Schuyler, May 29, 1781, Ibid., 92-93.

[107] RM to Washington, May 29, 1781, ibid., 94-96.

[108] Ibid., 96-98.

[109] Ibid., 153-154.

[110] RM to George Washington, June 21, 1781, ibid., 1:162.

[111] George Washington to RM, July 13, 1781, *The Writings of George Washington*, 22:365-367.

[112] RM to George Washington, *RM Papers*, 1:213-216.

[113] Ibid., July 5, 1781.

[114] RM Circular to the Several States, July 6, 1781, *RM Papers*, July 6, 1781.

[115] George Washington to Robert Morris, August 2, 1781, *The Writings of George Washington*, 22:450-451.

[116] Ibid.

[117] Diary: September 19, 1781, *RM Papers*, 2:297.

[118] From the Governor of North Carolina, August 4, 1781, *RM Papers*, 2:22.

[119] From Udny Hay [an agent], August 15, 1781, *RM Papers*, 2:61-63.

[120] From George Washington [to RM], August 17, 1781, *RM Papers*, 2:68-69.

[121] September 19, 1781, *RM Diary*, *RM Papers*, 2:297

[122] Certificates of foreign exchange were similar to letters of credit or bank checks drawn on a reliable foreign institution and payable in local currency.

[123] RM to the President of Congress [Elian Boudinot], January 24, 1783, *RM Papers*, 7:368.

[124] *RM Papers*, IX:688-698.

[125] George Washington to Jacob Read, November 3, 1784, Fitzpatrick, *Writings*, 27:489.

[126] GW to James Madison, November 30, 1785, PGW Confed., 3:419-421.

[127] Report of Proceedings in Congress, February 21, 1787, *Journals of the Continental Congress, 1774-1789*.

[128] RM to his sons, June 7, 1787, cited in Charles Henry Hart, *Mary White—Mrs. Robert Morris* (Philadelphia: An Address, *The Pennsylvania Magazine of History and Biography*, 1878), 170.

[129] RM to a Friend, January 1788, (Philadelphia: *The Pennsylvania Magazine of History and Biography*, II), 191-192.

1 G.W. Parke Custis, *Recollections and Private Memoirs of Washington* (Philadelphia: J. W. Bradley, 1861), 326.

[131] RM to Thomas Morris, April 2, 1802, in Charles Rappeleye, *Robert Morris: Financier of the American Revolution*, (New York: Simon & Schuster, 2010), 514.